CLIMB II:

Time to Soar

Teen and Young Adult Workbook

Individual use only. This book is not designed to be shared.

NAME

CLIMB II

Time to Soar
Teen and Young Adult Workbook

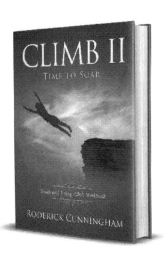

BY RODERICK C. CUNNINGHAM

A guide for teenagers and young adults to live their best life NOW!!

CLIMB II: Time to Soar

Teen and Young Adult Workbook by Roderick Cunningham

WORKBOOK USER LICENSE AGREEMENT

For customized training materials and/or to become a certified trainer of this material, contact Chief Empowerment Network, LLC directly at 813-380-8045.

Social/Emotional Training:

To book Mr. Cunningham directly for a keynote address, seminar, coaching or to train mentors, teachers, parents, law enforcement, or young people in your community about social/emotional wellness, please contact his team at info@rodcunninghamspeaks.com

Book Cover Layout: Valerie Cunningham

Book Cover Photos: Deposit Photos Credit: Bolina

Inside photography: Noah Diggs, Gibbs HS, St. Petersburg, FL

Inside Graphics: Meredith Rucker of Meredith Creative Marketing, Inc.

Edited by: Sheronne Burke, Valerie Cunningham, Erik Smith, and D. Simon

Conceptual Assistant: Dexter Wyckoff, II, Tampa, FL

Printed in the United States of America

ISBN-13:   978-17322659-12

ISBN-10:   1732265917

ABOUT THE AUTHOR

Rod Cunningham was born to a 15-year-old mother in the housing projects of Jacksonville, Florida. His father was 19-years-old when he died two weeks before his birth. Rod watched his step-father verbally and physically abuse his mother for 7 years, leading to he and his mother escaping the home in the middle of the night. They eventually divorced, leaving him to grow up without any adult male influence, which led to him having a daughter at 19-years-old, in search of his manhood. The choice to join the Air Force was the best decision of his life, getting plenty of male influence from men of honor, dignity, and character.

Rod retired from the U.S. Air Force after 29 years of dedicated service to our country in February 2016 as a Chief Master Sergeant (E-9). He developed leadership programs for the Air Force. In his role as Dean of Students, Air Force Technical Training School in Biloxi, MS, he personally counseled, mentored, and coached 2,500 students annually and developed a student mentorship program that decreased academic attrition rate by 90% in three years. After retirement, he joined the Pinellas County Urban League as Vice President of Corporate Relations where he successfully developed and managed a weekly poverty reduction program for 23 families in low-income communities.

He is currently a transformational speaker, youth empowerment coach, and community leader. He has participated in over 50 leadership and community panels, has delivered over 300 speeches and he is humbled by the fact that he has individually counseled, mentored, and empowered over 9,000 teenagers and young adults between the ages of 10 and 30 over the last six years who entrusted him with their innermost secrets. He mentors juvenile detainees, works with the Urban League's Youth and Empowerment Programs, developed and taught a manhood course for the Pinellas County Job Corps called "Confront and Conquer, The Journey to Manhood", and mentors 60+ young men and women each week.

Rod is regarded by many community leaders and young adults around the country as a leader who is passionate about the success of others. Rod speaks about facing your past to own your future. He has a simple, yet impactful way of showing how the events of life can put many of us in an emotional hole of varying degrees. Rod has the ability to, "get in the hole", because he's been there. He teaches you how to quickly CLIMB out before life's next major negative event. His techniques are designed to change a child, a family, a school, a community, a city, and a nation. Whether it is a one-on-one session, a 15-minute speech, a 1-hour speech, or a week-long seminar, Rod can help change the direction of your life!

Rod and his wife Valerie reside in the Tampa Bay Area of Florida. He has three adult children and five grandchildren.

Table of Contents

Acknowledgements

I feel a deep sense of gratitude to my family, friends, and clients for their assistance in completing this book. To my wife, Valerie, as in all things, you have been extremely supportive and understanding as I worked to complete this project. I appreciate your patience throughout the early mornings and late nights that I was focused on completing the book. Thank you for your patience and unconditional love. Our love is eternal.

To my three adult children, I appreciate you and the love that we share and continue to share as a family. Amber (Thomas Davis, SSG, U.S. Army), thank you for your constant love and communication. Dexter (Gianletty), thanks for your suggestions in helping to narrow the book's focus and for your public affairs advice. Erika, thank you for your love and support.

To the loving memory of my awesome Mother, Jacqui Granger of Jacksonville, FL (Sep 1952 – Dec 2014). You left us too soon. Your legacy and unconditional love will live on for generations. All that I am, I am because of your love, patience, and guidance. I humbly dedicate this book to you and your legacy.

To the happy memory of my wonderful Mother-In-Law, Cheryl Townsend of Tampa, FL, by way of Ft. Wayne, IN (Jan 1950 – May 2015). Thank you for your years of mentorship, love, and acceptance as a son. It was a joy learning from your life experiences. Thank you for encouraging me to write books.

To my extended family in Jacksonville, FL, Charlotte, NC, Atlanta, GA and Ft. Wayne, IN, thank you for your continued support over the years. Valerie and I appreciate your love.

To my fraternity brothers, of Omega Psi Phi Fraternity, Inc., thanks for your friendship.
-   My home chapter: Epsilon Mu Mu (MacDill Ques, Tampa, Florida)
-   My adopted chapters: Eta Rho (St. Petersburg, FL) / Iota Upsilon (Gulfport, MS)

"We can't allow life to take us over, we have to TAKE OVER our own lives. This requires a serious change in our daily routine."

- Rod Cunningham

Introduction

In my first book, *CLIMB: Face Your Past, Own Your Future*, I discuss how life's negative events can cause emotional isolation, which can put you in an emotional hole. Instead of looking at you in your hole and judging you for the bad decisions you may have made, or for shutting people out, I get in the hole with you because I recognize the hole. I am familiar with that hole. I was in that hole throughout my teenage years, and subsequently returned to a much deeper version of that hole in my mid 40's. It wasn't until I faced my past that I was able to own my future.

In the first book we discussed the Top 4 things that are bothering most teenagers: **Parental abandonment, loss of a loved one, trauma/abuse (sexual, physical, or verbal), and rejection by peers or significant others.**

The unfortunate truth is, if you go into an emotional hole at 14-years old, then you are still in it at 64-years-old if no one has taught you how to climb out. I revealed the five specific steps it takes to CLIMB out of your emotional hole.

This workbook, CLIMB II: Time to SOAR, teaches you how to soar by simply changing your daily routine. This successful daily routine has shown itself to be very successful for many. Most won't do what it takes to succeed, but if you have completed CLIMB I, then I know you are ready to SOAR beyond your wildest dreams. You may not know it, but today, right where you are, you have everything you need to be successful already inside of you, you just have to believe it.

Teachers/Counselors/School Psychologists:

CLIMB I, was designed to help you understand what is going on with the young person that you are responsible for during school hours. It helps you to understand a certain word, smell, taste, sound, or site may trigger an explosive reaction inside an otherwise calm classroom. Too many times we intervene *after* a child has an emotional outburst of anger or frustration instead of peeling back the onion to find the source.

CLIMB II is designed to help you and your students. Anyone can garner success from following the instructions in this manual. This book will help you to become a better mentor by getting your mentees on track early to pursue a successful life and career.

Community Mentors:

There are thousands of men and women who want to become mentors for our youth but don't know exactly how they can make a difference in the life of a teenager. CLIMB I will open the eyes of mentors and potential mentors around the world, and it will help you to connect with young people and hopefully give you some nuggets to connect with your own children, nieces, nephews, friends, and extended family members.

CLIMB II will guide you in providing help to any teenager who is looking for assistance in designing their future. This is the guide we wish our parents had when we were teenagers. Every happy, successful, and goal-oriented teenager is a win for all communities.

Parents:

CLIMB I was designed to help you understand what is really bothering your child, even when they don't know themselves. I wish I had this book when I raised three teenagers at the same time. The great thing about children is that they are resilient. It is never too late to hit the restart button when it comes to your children. Your children adore you and are looking for a reason to give you unconditional love. They just want you to love them and tell them that you are proud of them, no matter their age.

By reading CLIMB II for yourself, you will find it easier to guide your teenager and arm them with important information found in this book.

Teenagers/College Students/Young Adults: CLIMB I and CLIMB II are guides that you can use for the rest of your life. As a teenager, I did not have a father to guide my decision making, and my mother only knew what was taught to her. I would have loved to have reference guides to show me what to do when life got confusing.

CLIMB I and II should be read cover to cover more than once. They are designed as guides to be referenced daily, weekly, or monthly. If you follow the guidance and do what the books suggest, your life will NEVER be the same; I guarantee it!

Chapter 1

MY PERSONAL CLIMB AND HOW I SOARED

"Try to avoid complaints. Self-pity, even when legitimate, never fails to undermine your strength."

— Mariane Pearl

At 46-years-old I was at the top of my military career after spending 28 years serving my country. I was responsible for over 5,000 people annually, mostly between the ages of 18-25. My wife had multiple businesses and we were living a great life. Suddenly, my mother passed away from complications of influenza (the flu). My life stopped as I knew it. I didn't want to go to work, I was snappy and irritated most of the time, I had to fight the spirit of depression daily, I woke up between 2:30 and 3:00 am at least four times per week. I was an only child, my mother had me at the age of 15, and we had a very close and loving relationship. Although I traveled the world with the military, it never stopped my mom and I from talking at least 3-times per week (prior to cell phones). You can imagine my despair after she died suddenly. I started playing 3 to 4 hours of mobile gaming each day to escape my life. I was upset with my extended family because no one called to check on me after the first 2 weeks of burying my mother, however, they called when they wanted the stuff she left behind (car, furniture, jewelry, purses, etc.).

In my position as Dean of Students, Air Force Technical Training School, I counseled/coached over 2,500 students each year. There is nothing more humbling than having 9,000+ individuals open up and share their deepest emotional hurts with you. Upon referring the students to higher levels of professional counseling, I was pleased to see an improvement in their performance.

Once I began to struggle with my life after my mom's death, I knew what I needed to do to get better, but I just didn't feel like doing those things at the time. I knew that I needed to speak with a psychologist, just as I had referred thousands of others. I felt that I would somehow dishonor my mother's legacy if I stopped thinking about the pain of her dying, instead of enjoying and celebrating the memories we shared.

Setting up an Air Force mental health appointment was actually quite easy, although I procrastinated a few months before I went into action. While in the waiting room the receptionist gave me a survey to see how I was feeling that day.

> *"Did you sleep well last night? Are you feeling tired and hopeless? Do you feel worthless? Do you feel as though you want to hurt yourself or others?"*

The psychologist greeted me in the lobby, walked me to his office, then said, "Chief, what would you like to talk about"? I said, "Doc, my mom died two months ago, I wake up at 3:00 am at least 4 nights per week, I'm irritable and snappy towards my wife, my mother-in-law lives with me and has Stage 4 Lung Cancer and is currently hospitalized in the intensive care unit at the base hospital, and my wife is worried and concerned about me and her mother. So, what should I do?" I also shared that whenever I visited my mother-in-law, the hospital equipment noise made me nervous because it reminded me of when my mom died in the intensive care unit.

As you can see, I was unbalanced with a broken heart, and was in a deep emotional hole. My life had been turned upside down in a very short period of time. It was unreal for me. The great thing for me, however, was that I knew I was in an emotional hole, and although I knew how to get out, at the time I didn't feel like doing what was necessary to CLIMB out.

Five months after my mom died, my mother-in-law passed away. Her death plunged me even deeper in the hole as I was very close to my mother-in-law. I also had to deal with the deep emotional hurt my wife was experiencing. During this period my psychologist asked if I wanted to see a psychiatrist who could prescribe me anti-depressant medication. Although I was in an emotional hole and knew what I needed to do to climb out, I was curious to see what the psychiatrist would say. As I sat with the psychiatrist, he seemed a lot more formal than my psychologist. He listened to me talk, then asked if I wanted him to prescribe me an anti-depressant. I refused the medicine and continued my counseling sessions with the psychologist.

Although my psychologist was very helpful to me because I needed to vent and be very transparent about my feelings, I felt as though he didn't give me the "detailed" advice or guidance that I needed at the time. I needed more instructions on "what to do next". The sessions were limited to one hour and I was only allowed about 6 sessions before an evaluation occurred to see if the psychologist would continue to see me.

Personally, I feel that the mental health professionals should add life coaching as a follow-up to psychologists. While psychologists can help you to come to grips with what happened in your past, a life coach focuses on helping you to design an awesome future, both personally and professionally. A good life coach will empower you and hold you accountable for living your best life now. It is my opinion that primary care physicians should be able to write a prescription for coaching.

HOW I SOARED
Here are some of the things I began to do immediately while I was still in counseling:

1. I prayed every morning and my wife encouraged me to read specific verses in the Bible.

2. I listened to four different spiritual/motivational messages per day by Pastor Joel Osteen and Bishop T.D. Jakes on satellite radio and YouTube.

3. I found purpose in my life through helping young people (aged 14-35) climb out of their emotional holes, and by mentoring enlisted personnel, officers, and teens at juvenile detention centers around Mississippi where I was stationed.

4. I forgave everyone in my life who hurt me or disappointed me.

Before retiring from the Air Force with 29 years of service, I was still experiencing bouts of sadness about once every few weeks or so. It had been 12 months since my mother's death and seven since my mother-in-law's death. I was taught that if you are still sad from the death of a loved one after 30 days (Numbers 20:29 and Deuteronomy 34:8), then you will need external emotional help to remove the negative emotions from the thought of that loved one. In other words, I should not still cry when I talked about or thought about my mother. Conversely, the thought of both mothers should bring a smile to my face. Thinking of them should not invoke fear, anxiety, sadness, grief, anger, or guilt. Rather, it should inspire me to celebrate how they lived while they were here on earth.

A few months after moving back to the Tampa Bay area (December 2015), I started listening heavily to motivational messages from Les Brown, Tony Robbins, and Eric Thomas. Once I began to understand and apply their messages, I went on a more advanced journey of self-discovery by studying the works of Bob Proctor. I did not take a job for 12 months after retirement, instead I volunteered to work with the youth in St. Petersburg, FL and began building relationships with schools, community residents, and community leaders. I began a daily routine to develop a healthy mind, a healthy body, and a healthy spirit. So productive was this routine that I was approached by community leaders to come out of retirement and accept a leadership position. So, within months of moving to St.

Petersburg, the St. Petersburg Police Chief, President/CEO of the Pinellas County Urban League, and a County Commissioner all approached me about high-level leadership positions. I don't say these things to boast, but my point is that my new daily routine of visualization, positive thinking, and positive action created a mutual attraction between me and these community leaders. (I will talk more about this routine later in this book).

Although this book stands alone in its ability to help you soar, if you follow the recommendations in both CLIMB and CLIMB II, you will not be able to recognize yourself in as little as 12 months. Also, I suggest that you invest in yourself by taking the time to learn about Neurolinguistics Programming (NLP) and Time Line Therapy® (Dr. Tad James)[01]. They both really helped me take full control of my thoughts and my reactions to things in my life that may have had me angry or sad in the past.

We take in information through our five senses: Touch, smell, taste, hearing, and sight. Our mind then processes this information based on our values, beliefs, decisions, and memories. We then ingest the information and determine how we (our mind) will decide to use it. This ingestion and assimilation of information gives us our "personal" internal representation (what it means to us) which is then activated by sounds, feelings, pictures, smells, tastes, etc. For example, if I wake up because I *smell* smoke, my mind processes the information based on my memory that wherever there is smoke, there is fire. My personal internal representation displays a picture in my head of a fire, so I jump out of bed to investigate. If I had never smelled smoke before, then I would not respond with the same urgency, I would simply go back to sleep. If I had never smelled smoke before I may even justify my inaction to my spouse by saying, "I didn't get out of bed because I didn't think anything was wrong because I have never smelled smoke before." I might even say, "Where I am from, people use burn pits all the time to stay warm, so I figured it was the neighbors burn pit."

To continue with the smelling smoke example, one person may jump out of bed to investigate the smell while the other may stay in bed because they don't think it is anything serious. In this example actuality, a fire was actually burning in the walls of the kitchen due to an electrical issue. One person acted on it while the other didn't; but there was still a fire.

Let's look at another example. Two brothers ages 8 and 9 lose their father in a car accident. One brother grows up to be an alcoholic, the other a workaholic and verbal abuser. One brother realizes that their father's death is causing him to act out and make bad decisions so he takes action to CLIMB by getting counseling, forgiving his father for leaving him, and developing a strong spiritual life. Just because the other brother says "I'm fine" while continuing to make bad decisions doesn't mean that his bad decision making is not related to his father's death. The fact is that one brother acted, while the other ignored it, "but the house was still on fire".

SPIRITUAL REFERENCE:

"Haven't I commanded you? Strength! Courage! Don't be timid; don't get discouraged. God, your God, is with you every step you take."
- **Joshua 1:9 (MSG)**

FAMOUS QUOTE:

"You can't stay in your corner of the Forest waiting for others to come to you. You have to go to them sometimes."
- **A.A. Milne**

TAKEAWAYS:

1. If you don't take action, your life will remain the same or get worse.

2. We should remove negative emotions from past events by learning something positive from those events. Now when we think of that event, we smile in victory.

3. When you find yourself in a difficult situation, simply ask, "If I didn't believe it was impossible, what could I do about it?

AFFIRMATIONS: *(Recite each morning)*

I am strong and I live in victory every day.

TIME TO SOAR:

Exercise 1: DAILY MOTIVATION

Materials needed: Smart Phone / YouTube App

It is important for our brains to hear positive, uplifting messages each day. A dose of motivation each day can help you achieve your daily goals and it creates a positive mindset.

1. Choose a motivational speaker below and go to YouTube and search for their names

    - Les Brown (Speaker)
    - Eric Thomas (Speaker)
    - Tony Robbins (Life Coach)
    - TD Jakes (Spiritual Leader)
    - Joel Osteen (Spiritual Leader)
    - Bob Proctor (Life Coach - Advanced Mental Concepts)

2. Listen to at least a 20-minute motivational message each day. Listening to the same message over multiple days can be very effective.

Chapter 2

CLIMB: FACE YOUR PAST, OWN YOUR FUTURE

"The best years of your life are the ones in which you decide your problems are your own. You do not blame them on your mother, the ecology, or the president. You realize that you control your own destiny."

– Albert Ellis

As discussed in *CLIMB: Face Your Past, Own Your Future*, when you are 8 years old and your parents get a divorce, you fall into an emotional hole, and you don't know it. When you are 12 years old and you visit your angry father, who hits you for lying to him, although you didn't lie, you fall deeper into that same emotional hole because you don't "feel" unconditional love from your biological father and you don't feel as though he is proud of you. When you are 16-years-old your grandmother passes away, because you felt that your grandmother was the only person that that truly understood you, loved you unconditionally and consistently told you that she was proud of you, you find yourself even deeper in that hole. When your best friend is killed in a car accident during your senior year in high school, you fall even deeper in that same emotional hole. Then, when you are 28-years-old you get a divorce from the person that you thought you'd be with for the rest of your life, and that person tries to take your children away from you, you fall even deeper in that hole.

At this point, most of your family and friends will simply look down in your hole and make comments like,

"Why are you still talking about that?"
"You need to let that go"
"What is wrong with you?"
"Get over it!"
"Your father hit you 15 years ago, move on."

"Take that outside and bury it for once and for all"
"Are you crazy?"
"Just pray about it"

Unfortunately, no one teaches you HOW to CLIMB out of the hole.

If you are to move forward with your life effectively, you must take a hard look at where you've come from. Our childhood shapes our adulthood, whether we realize it or not. Here are the Top 4 things that are bothering most teenagers:

1. You don't have the relationship with one of your biological parents that you DESIRE to have. **(ABANDONMENT)**

2. Someone who you truly loved has passed away (i.e., sibling, parent, grandparent, uncle, aunt, significant other, cousin, best friend, etc.) **(LOSS)**

3. You were physically assaulted, verbally abused, or touched inappropriately by someone older than you. Additionally, you may have been abused by law enforcement or witnessed abuse of a loved one. **(ABUSE/TRAUMA)**

4. Rejected by your peers or significant other. **(REJECTION)**

In the book **CLIMB: Face Your Past, Own Your Future**, we discuss a set of five strategies to help you or a loved one out of emotional isolation. If we live long enough, we will all experience emotional isolation or as I like to call it, the emotional hole. The emotional hole is not a negative thing. It is just how I describe it to create a picture of how abandonment, loss, trauma, and rejection creates levels of emotional pain that if not dealt with properly, can lead to even deeper and more frequent emotional pain. We then reach for something to comfort us when we are stressed or when the trauma is triggered. If we associate with people who choose the same comfort (i.e. alcohol, food, drugs, etc.) we view our behavior as normal.

The presence of LOVE and acceptance makes a large difference in our emotions, which normally drives our decision-making process. Here are examples of positive and negative emotions:

1. Positive Emotions: Happiness, joy, gratitude, serenity, hope, pride, inspiration, kindness, amusement, cheerfulness, and LOVE

2. Negative Emotions: Sadness, anger, anxiety, guilt, grief, and despair

LOVE CONQUERS ALL

Everyone wants to be loved. If you ask 10 people to define love you will get 10 different answers. We all want love, but very few of us know how to give love.

Love is patient, love is kind. It does not envy, it does not boast, it is not proud. It does not dishonor others, it is not self-seeking, it is not easily angered, it keeps no record of wrongs. Love does not delight in evil but rejoices with the truth. It always protects, always trusts, always hopes, always perseveres. [02]

Love is a daily "action" we take to show someone how much we care about them.

What is unconditional love? It is an affection that does not have conditions or limitations. Many consider it complete love as it has no bounds and is unchanging. It is a term used between couples in highly committed relationships, between close friends, and between family members.

Most importantly, it separates the individual from his or her behaviors.

What is conditional love? Love that is earned. "If you do this for me, then I will love you."

Love should never have to be earned. Love is a grace that we give each other. We can love every human being in the world unconditionally if we realize that we all are doing the best that we can do based on how we were raised.

Unconditional love is a long-term **_choice_** and promise that we make **_daily_** to commit a heartfelt, kind, and *caring action toward a person that is imperfect*.

Can we all agree that everyone wants to be loved unconditionally? We all want to be loved just as we are, we don't want to feel as though we need to change in order for others to accept us.

At 14 years old we want to know that our biological parents are there to help us navigate life. We feel as though they should understand us best because we are descendants of them. When one parent is tired, irritated or too busy to engage us, we want the ability to go to the other parent for love, comfort, and understanding. This is in no way to discount the role of a step-parent or adoptive parent. It is simply to help you understand what our natural emotional needs are as human beings.

Once the 14-year-old has the stability of love and comfort from parents, then he is free to develop healthy relationships with friends and classmates. Adolescents may not engage parents often at this age, but knowing that parents are proud, available, supportive, and demonstrates their support by attending sporting and school events are important aspects of the parent-child relationship.

Refer to *CLIMB: Face Your Past, Own Your Future* for the five steps to CLIMB out of the emotional hole. Psychologically speaking, we want you to start with a healthy, balanced emotional state of mind as we move into CLIMB II.

SPIRITUAL REFERENCE:

> *"My beloved friends, let us continue to love each other since love comes from God. Everyone who loves is born of God and experiences a relationship with Him..."*

- 1 John 4:7 (MSG)

FAMOUS QUOTE:

> *"I saw that you were perfect, and so I loved you. Then I saw that you were not perfect and I loved you even more."*

- Angelita Lim

TAKEAWAYS:

1. Everyone deserves to be loved unconditionally because we are simply imperfect humans.

2. Top 4 things bothering teenagers:
   a. Not having the relationship that you desire to have with a biological parent (ABANDONEMENT)
   b. Death of a friend or loved one (LOSS)
   c. Physical/verbal abuse and/or inappropriate touching (ABUSE/TRAUMA)
   d. Bullying or rejection from a friend or significant other (REJECTION)

3. We all want to know two things from our biological parents:
   a. Do you love me unconditionally?
   b. Are you proud of me?

AFFIRMATIONS: *(Recite each morning)*

1. I will tell my parents that I love them unconditionally every day.
2. I will LOVE everyone unconditionally.
3. I will communicate often with my parents and inform them of my need to be loved and supported.

TIME TO SOAR:

Exercise 1: UNCONDITIONAL LOVE

Materials needed: Cell phone

1. List the names of the people who LOVES YOU unconditionally (just like you are):

   _____

   _____

   _____

   _____

2. List the names of the people who YOU LOVE unconditionally (just like they are):

   _____

   _____

   _____

   _____

3. Both lists should match. If they don't match, please explain why?

   _____

   _____

   _____

   Remember, every human being deserves to be loved unconditionally. We don't have to agree with their choices or their behavior, but we should love them nonetheless.

"True adulthood occurs the moment we grasp that the people who raised us do not exist solely for our comfort and reassurance. From that point on, the steady stream of unconditional love and support we've expected from them all our lives has to flow both ways."

- Lynn Coady

Chapter 3

TIME TO GROW UP

"Maturity: Be able to stick with a job until it is finished. Be able to bear an injustice without having to get even. Be able to carry money without spending it. Do your duty without being supervised."

- Ann Landers

Children can't wait to become adults and adults wish they could become children again because life can be very stressful and demanding. Making important life decisions, paying bills, raising children, balancing time with your church/community, buying homes and cars, trying to keep a successful romantic relationship, and the demands of corporate America, the military, and/or running a business can really wear anyone down.

I hear many teenagers say that they can't wait until they turn 18 years old so that they can move out and live by their own rules. Because most 18-year-olds are making less than $11 per hour, in most situations, it would take many roommates to be able to afford rent, utilities, cable, and food.

Here's a sample monthly breakdown (with 2 roommates in Florida):

Rent (your portion): $400

Electric (your portion): $60

Water (your portion): $30

Internet/cable (your portion): $50

Food for you (breakfast-$5/lunch-$8/Dinner-$12): $750

Cell phone: $50

Transportation (i.e. gas, bus, etc.): $100

Toiletries: $50

Total Bills and Expenses: **$1,490.00**

Full-time monthly salary @ $11.00 per hour:

$1,760 – 20% for income taxes ($352) = **$1,408**

Negative $82 per month is your situation. You have no money for a car, insurance, or entertainment. Oh, and please don't start having children under this kind of economic stress.

What do you do now?

1. Do you borrow that money from your parents, grandparents, aunt, uncle, or siblings? How long do you make others responsible for your decisions?

2. Do you live within your means by cutting back on food costs and eating oatmeal and noodles @ $2 a meal?

3. Do you get an additional job where you now work 12-16 hours a day and/or 7 days per week?

4. Do you move out, jump from house to house staying on a friend's couch until they get tired of you and you eventually start sleeping in your car?

5. Do you move out of your place with your roommate, quit your job, go back home and quietly stay in your parents' home playing video games, listening to music, and interacting with social media all day? This is until your parents get tired and put you out or demand you go to work.

6. Do you go back home to live with parents and enroll in a community college or a technical school to gain knowledge and skills that leads to higher pay, distancing yourself from other unskilled workers and making yourself more marketable?

7. Do you join the military where they will give you a similar starting salary and provide you with food, clothing, and shelter?

8. Do you buckle down, get focused, enroll in a college/university, find scholarships and grants, and begin working on your Bachelor's Degree?

These are the life/career choices that 18 to 25-year-olds are facing every day. Historically speaking, young men feel the most pressure to succeed at this age. They have been taught that men are protectors and providers and that *"A man that doesn't work, doesn't eat."* That pressure is accentuated in relationships as well. Our significant others often tell men to *"grow up"* or *"man up"*, and when we ask for clarification, they say *"you should know"*.

Depending on the context and the situation, here's what I think it means when a girlfriend or wife says, *"grow up"*:

1. Get a job and pay some bills.
2. Stop being offended or jealous of my friendships with others.
3. Stop sleeping on your friend's couch.
4. Put down the video games and focus your attention on me and the kids.
5. Do your homework and stop trying to cheat your way out of high school or college.
6. Pay your child support.
7. Spend time with ALL of your children.
8. Read more so that you can gain wisdom to pass down to your children.
9. Keep your promises
10. Tell the truth at all times.
11. Stop quitting jobs before you get a new one.
12. Stop working dead end jobs and go back to school for a career.

13. Come home at a decent hour.

14. Stop abusing alcohol or drugs and get some help like you promised.

15. Don't complain or blame everyone else for your problems.

16. Don't fight, get angry, or walk away when someone disagrees with you.

17. Deal with your emotions and stop sleeping with other girls to make you feel better about yourself.

18. Get in touch with your spiritual life.

19. Stop yelling and using profanity to win arguments, you are smarter than that.

20. When you see something is broken in the house, pull out your toolbox and fix it.

21. Practice good hygiene (i.e. take a bath, brush your teeth, wash your hair, etc.)

22. Treat your parents with respect.

23. There are people that care about you, don't mistreat them.

24. If you won't listen to me, find a mentor.

25. Stop buying what you WANT and begging for money from others for what you NEED.

26. Finish your education so that you can provide a better life for your family.

27. Stop putting your friends before your family.

28. Stop allowing distractions to overtake you, take control over your life.

29. Respect your parents and I can have confidence that you will respect me.

30. Show honesty, character, loyalty and integrity. If you lie to others, one day you will lie to me.

Speaking to the males here, as you can see, when you become an adult, the list above will be expected from your significant other. Your significant other has more expectations of you than your parents had while you were growing up. Take a look at the table below. It provides basic attributes of a successful adult that is expected by the community in which you live.

Young ladies and young men, check all of the boxes below that makes you feel excited about becoming an adult:

Table 3-1

	Developing **Independence**	Takes full financial/physical responsibility for your home, your bills, your car, your cellphone, your spouse, and your children, ALL of your children. No one should pay these things on your behalf.
	Dating and marrying someone who shows **Love and Respect**	Find someone who loves and respects you and ensure that you love and respect them back.
	Showing **Unconditional Love** to others	Show unconditional love to your spouse, children, and parents. Don't put conditions on your love.
	Showing **Character** (Keeping your word)	Someone with good intentions will make you a promise, someone with good character will keep that promise.
	Developing a **Solid Work Ethic**	You must develop a habit of GIVING MORE than what you are paid to do. You should always go above and beyond what is required of you at your job and the organizations that you are a part of.
	Developing a strong **Spiritual Life**	Develop a faith walk. We all have a spirit inside of us, whether we believe it or not, and if we are to live a fulfilled life, we are to feed that spirit with spiritual food (i.e. listening to spiritual music, listening to spiritual messages, attending spiritual events, being kind and loving others, reading spiritual books, etc.) You don't have to believe what I believe but believe in something greater than yourself!
	Accepting Responsibility for my actions and the actions of my family.	Don't blame others for your problems. OWN YOUR MESS! Once you take responsibility for yourself and your family's actions, only then can change occur. If everyone sits back and point fingers, then they can relax and stop thinking of solutions because it is someone else's mess to fix.

	Eating Healthy and Exercising (i.e. weightlifting, team sports, running, biking, boxing, etc.)	Exercise and eat properly to extend your life and relieve stress, because stress causes diseases like cancer and high blood pressure. Do what you can to live a long, prosperous life.
	Displaying **Good Hygiene**	Take baths daily, brush and floss your teeth, keep your hair washed and cleaned, get a haircut, and clean your nose/ears often.
	Showing **Accountability**	Never give in to peer pressure, watch who influences you, choose good friends, monitor your circle, and do not release anger on people you love.
	Showing **kindness**, **good manners**, and **respect** to others	Kindness, manners, and respect doesn't cost anything. It is a reflection of your environment, upbringing, and how you see the world. People are willing to help you succeed when you are respectful and kind.
	Showing **Dependability**	People love knowing that they can depend on someone to help them and be there for them when needed.
	Being **Honest**	Tell the truth. People want to know that they can depend on you to be honest with them. Show kindness and respect when you are being honest.
	Having **faith**	Faith is the confidence or trust in a person or thing. We are not in total control of our lives. We must have faith or be aligned with a belief system where we know that we will receive the desires of our hearts, if that is the plan for OUR lives.
	Being **Loyal**	Loyalty is a strong feeling of support or allegiance. One can be loyal to their spouse, children, parents, friends, employer, religion, community, country, etc.

QUESTIONS:

1. What excites you most about becoming an adult?

    _____

    _____

2. Do you currently pay ALL of your own bills (including cell phone and car insurance)?
    YES | NO

3. Do you respect and love the person or persons who help you or who pays all or most of your bills? How often do you thank them for their sacrifice in helping you?

    _____

4. Are you respectful and are you dating or married to someone who shows respect to you, your parents, and everyone else?

    _____

5. Are you a dependable person?

    _____

6. If you have children, are you emotionally, physically, and financially responsible for ALL of their lives and for their success in the future?

    _____

7. Is someone else, outside of the biological mother/father providing the emotional, physical, and financial responsibility for your child? How often have you thanked them for their sacrifice in helping you provide for your child?

    _____

    _____

SPIRITUAL REFERENCE:

"When I was a child, I talked like a child, I thought like a child, I reasoned like a child. When I became a man, I put the ways of childhood behind me."
- ***1 Corinthians 13:11 (NIV)***

FAMOUS QUOTE:

"Growing up in a group home, and with an undiagnosed learning disability to boot, the odds of success were not on my side. But when I joined the high school football team, I learned the value of discipline, focus, persistence, and teamwork - all skills that have proven vital to my career as a C.E.O. and social entrepreneur."
- ***Darell Hammond***

TAKEAWAYS:

1. You have the rest of your life to be grown, enjoy being a child.

2. Be patient with your parents and their rules. You will likely follow some sort of rule or system designed by someone else (i.e. corporate rules, college rules, dorm rules, military rules, state laws, traffic laws, house rules when living with others, etc.). If you resist rules and structure, it may not be the rule that you are resisting, but it may be emotional stress caused by past events from your childhood (i.e. trauma, abandonment, etc.) or very recent emotional events (i.e. loss, rejection, etc.).

3. Avoid becoming a parent too early, it will cause unnecessary stress on you and your parents. Stress causes us to reach for something to comfort us (i.e. alcohol, drugs, video games, food, cigarettes, etc.).

4. Take full responsibility for yourself and your children.

5. Show appreciation for anyone who provides financial, emotional, or physical support for you and/or your child.

AFFIRMATIONS: *(Recite each morning)*

1. I will show appreciation to anyone who actively supports me and/or my family.
2. I will take responsibility for my choices.
3. I will only blame myself for the direction of my life.

TIME TO SOAR:

Exercise 1: COST TO LIVE (Age 14 and Up)

Materials needed: Paper, pencil, and smartphone

1. Determine the median income for an ***unskilled*** 18 to 21-year-old in your area. Call a friend between 18-21 years old who makes good money and ask them about their hourly salary, skills needed to do the job, their position title, company name and how long have they been working there. Let them know that this is a survey for a course that you are taking. Be careful, it can be considered rude to ask someone what they earn.

   Highest Pay: $_____ per hour **OR** $_____ per month

   Number of hours worked per week: _____

   Company Name: _____

   Position Title: _____

   How many months in this position? _____

   Is the company owned by them or a family member?_**YES / NO**

   Lowest Pay: $_____ per hour **OR** $_____ per month

   Number of hours worked per week: _____

   Company Name: _____

   Position Title: _____

   How many months in this position? _____

   Is the company owned by them or a family member?_**YES / NO**

2. Look on the internet and call your favorite apartment complex and ask the following questions:

Rent for a Studio Apt: $____

Rent for a one-bedroom apt: $_____

Rent for a two-bedroom apt: $_____

Rent for a three-bedroom apt: $_____

Average electric bill: $_____

Average water bill: $_____

Average internet costs: $_____

Average cable costs: $_____

$_____TOTAL *Housing/Utilities Costs*

3. Figure out the cost of food:

Breakfast daily (whether you purchase it or make it yourself): $_____

Lunch daily (whether you purchase it or make it yourself): $_____

Dinner daily (whether you purchase it or make it yourself): $_____

How much for buying coffee or eating at a restaurant: $_____

$_____TOTAL *Food Costs*

4. Figure out the cost of toiletries each month: Total $_____

Toothpaste: $_____   Mouthwash: $ _____   Soap: $_____
Shampoo: $_____   Vitamins: $ _____   Deodorant: $ _____
Toilet Paper: $_____   Hair Products: $_____   Women's personal items: $_____

$_____TOTAL *Toiletry Costs*

5. Now, take a moment to figure out how many times you get your hair done monthly, how much to get your laundry done at a laundromat, how much will you pay monthly for furniture, clothing, shoes, cell phone, transportation and entertainment.

$_____TOTAL *Barber and/or Beauty Salon*

$_____TOTAL *Laundry Costs*

$_____TOTAL Monthly Costs for *Furniture*

$_____TOTAL Monthly Costs for *Clothing, Shoes, and Undergarments*

$_____TOTAL Monthly *Cell Phone* Costs

$_____TOTAL Monthly *Transportation* Costs (bus, gas, insurance, car payment)

$_____TOTAL Monthly *Entertainment* Costs (novels, movie subscriptions, music subscriptions, dinner with friends, partying with friends, feeding friends who visit your home, traveling, theme parks, movie night, etc.)

6. When stressed, we look for something to **comfort** us. The things we choose for comfort are usually things that we buy or are costly to partake in. These things can cost us money, time (which we can never get back), or a friendship/romantic relationship.
$_____TOTAL Monthly COMFORT Costs (i.e. alcohol, drugs, pornography, clubbing, cigarettes, video games, excessive shopping, potato chips and chocolate, gambling, sexual addiction, etc.)

GRAND TOTAL OF MONTHLY

BILLS/EXPENSES: $ _____ x 12 = $ _____ Annual Expenses

TOTAL MONTHLY INCOME: $_____ x 12 = $_____ Annual Pay

7. If your monthly income can't support your projected or actual bills/expenses, then what are you willing to do about it?

	Go to a college/university after high school for Bachelor's Degree (allow scholarships, grants, and student loans to pay for college and support me)
	Go to a community college for an associate's degree if not accepted at a 4-year college/university
	Join the military after high school
	Enroll in a technical college/trade school while in high school or immediately after high school graduation
	Get a second job
	Find enough roommates to split all costs and get a larger house/apartment
	Find a mentor, counselor, or life coach who will help me design my future
	Live with my parents until I'm 30-years-old
	Get married and let my spouse take care of me
	Start having children out-of-wedlock and let the government take care of me
	I will take NO ACTION at all. I will keep on living and see what happens.

This exercise is not designed to scare you, but to help you understand what it takes to make a living in today's world. Get a wise mentor quickly. Many times, when we can't talk to our parents, we normally go to our grandparents, aunt, uncle, pastor, coach, teacher, etc. Listen to them and allow them to guide you into becoming an adult that your community would be proud of. Don't ruin a mentor/coach relationship by asking for money. Knowledge is 10 times more valuable than money. If you are too emotional to listen to the advice of a wise man or woman, you are headed for a troubled life. Listen, listen, listen, then put some action behind what you have learned.

Chapter 4

DEVELOP YOURSELF

"Maturity: Be able to stick with a job until it is finished. Be able to bear an injustice without having to get even. Be able to carry money without spending it. Do your duty without being supervised."

- Ann Landers

There are certain ACTIONS that a person can take to develop themselves and live their best lives. Some people learn how to take advantage of self-development in their teen years, while others either figure it out in their 50's or they never figure it out.

To become successful in your personal, professional, and spiritual life, you must do the following for self-development:

Table 4-1

	Find a Mentor	Ask someone who has achieved what you want to achieve and schedule lunch with them once or twice monthly. Be sure that you pay for their meal. It is the mentee's responsibility to keep the relationship strong. Come to the mentorship session with a plan and allow your mentor to teach you how to execute that plan faster while stressing the importance of building strong relationships.
	Forgive Yourself and Forgive Others who may have hurt you in the past	Thoughts become things. You must begin to speak positive about today and your future. Unforgiveness, sadness, and anger will keep you bound to negative thoughts from your past.
	Develop a Vision Board	Search for pictures of careers, houses, families, cars, vacations, and the lifestyle that you want to have within the next 2-20 years. Paste those images on a poster board and hang it on your wall to be looked at daily. (See Chapter 9 for details)

	Develop an attitude of gratitude	Write down the 15 things that you are most grateful for and read it daily when you wake up. (See Book 2 for a sample list)
	Develop 15-20 Daily Affirmations	The affirmations should start with "I am …" (See Book 2 for a sample list)
	Develop short and long-term goals	Short-term (6 months – 1 year) and long-term (1-15 years) goals should be developed. Develop Professional/Educational, Spiritual, and Personal goals. (See Book 2 for a sample list)
	Manage Expectations w/everyone you love	Ask your parents, "What do you expect from me as your son or daughter?" After they tell you, then you say "Now can I tell you what I expect from you as my parents?" Ask this question to your friends, supervisors, spouse, siblings, etc.
	Develop Your Mind Daily	You can tell a person's intelligence by the books in their library. Reading motivational books and listening to speakers can help keep your mind sharp and focused on your dreams and goals. It can also open you up to the possibilities of all that life has to offer.
	Accept Responsibility for the Good and Bad in your life	Don't blame others for the things that happen in your life. When you take responsibility, you are telling yourself that you can actually fix the situation or possibly prevent it from happening again.
	Create Four Personal Pillars of Trust	Create four people in your life that you will consult in times of turmoil. (i.e. Mom, dad, aunt, uncle, pastor, coach, teacher, grandparent, attorney, mentor, mature friend, spouse, sibling, etc.)
	Formal Education	Associates, Bachelor's, and Master's Degrees will help to build on your intellect, your confidence, expose you to knowledge and information, as well as a system of successful people (network) that can help catapult you and help you to live your best life.

	Become an Avid Reader	If you read 2 books per week for 2 years on any subject, you would become the subject matter expert. You could possibly have more knowledge than a person with a Master's Degree in the same subject area.
	Become a Saver/Investor and not a Spender	Learn to pay yourself first after you take care of your religious/charitable obligations of 10%. Pay yourself 20% of your income with 10% going into a retirement account/10% going into savings for a rainy day. Fight the urge to buy a large house or expensive car until you can afford to pay at least half of the cost in cash.
	Feed your spirit man	We all have a spirit whether we believe or accept it or not, it is there. In order to live a better life, we must do things to feed the spirit man that is inside of us. We feed it by listening to spiritual music, listening to sermons, reading the Bible or your preferred spiritual book, helping people, being kind to people, and attending a spiritual service, just to name a few.

QUESTIONS:

1. Do you have a mentor? Yes | No | I'm Looking for One

2. Do you think that it is OK to have multiple mentors? Yes | No | Maybe

3. Why is forgiveness important?

   _____

   _____

4. Do you think visualizing your future can be helpful? Yes | No
   Why or why not?

   _____

   _____

5. Why is it important to be a person of character?

   _____

   _____

6. Do you have professional/educational, spiritual, and personal goals? Are they written down? Do you review them at least twice per day?

   _____

   _____

7. Do you ever use the term, "It's your fault" or "It's Not Fair"?
   Yes | No | Sometimes

8. How many self-development books have you read weekly?

   _____

9. Who is responsible for your SUCCESS in High School, College and in LIFE?

	My teachers
	My parents
	My siblings
	My significant other
	Law enforcement officers
	The mayor
	The government (i.e., free grants, welfare, etc.)
	The economy (i.e., more jobs)
	I AM

10. Who has the power to derail your success and stop you from achieving your goals?

	My teachers
	My parents
	My siblings
	My significant other

	Law enforcement officers
	The mayor
	The government (i.e., free grants, welfare, etc.)
	The economy (i.e., more jobs)
	Me

11. Do you plan to attend college? Why or why not?

_____

_____

12. Do you save your money or do you spend it as soon as you get it?

_____

_____

YOUR CHARACTER

"Nearly all men can stand adversity, but if you want to test a man's character, give him power."

- Abraham Lincoln

When we allow ourselves to get stressed, we normally reach for something to make us feel better, something to comfort us. This is how vices are created. Some vices are destructive and involve illegal activity like drugs, while others are harmful to our relationships like excessive video gaming or shutting others out through emotional isolation. In both situations, we may find ourselves struggling in relationships with our children, spouse, parents, best friend, and/or supervisor.

Although we may not always make the best decisions, it important to note our good qualities and began to build on those qualities.

Your Good Qualities

The list below are some important qualities of someone who has a good heart: (Check all that apply to you currently)

Table 4-2

Shows empathy	Says words like, - *"I don't know what to say to you, but I am glad you shared your pain with me. I am here if you need me"*. - *"Let me help you. I've been in the same hole that you are in and I am willing to get in with you."*
Shows sympathy	Says words like "I'm sorry your dog died, BUT you can always get a new dog." They are concerned for a moment, then life must go on. I prefer empathy over sympathy.
Good manners	Will hold doors for others, speak or wave to people in passing, and respects the space and belongings of others.
Shows kindness	Places phone call often to check on friends and family.
Responsive to others	Responds to emails, texts, or phone calls in a timely manner.

Shows love to others	Tells parents, friends, siblings, and the important people in their life that they love them prior to getting off the phone or leaving their presence.
Respectful of others	Use words like, "Excuse me" and "May I."
Respectful of authority	Uses words like, "Yes Ma'am," or "Yes Sir."
Donates time to causes	Volunteers in the community.
Willing to help a person in need	Will give someone a ride if they see them walking or at a bus stop.
Listens to the needs of others	Listens to others without interrupting them.
Cares about what happens to others	Will call a friend to check to see if they are OK after a sickness.
Able to keep secrets of others	Will not spread gossip about someone else who maybe experiencing problems in their life.
Looks for ways to help and/or mentor others	Will go out of their way to mentor others by volunteering to help them become successful in life and in business.
Grateful attitude	Uses words like, "Thank you, please, and I appreciate you."
Dependable	Shows up at work and to meetings on time.
Does what they say	Keeps their word.
Good Character	Honest, courageous, loyal, ethical, and lives by a moral code.
Honorable	Strives to live a life worth emulating and respects our military and law enforcement. Believes in truth and fairness.
Shows Integrity	They will always do what is right, even when no one else is looking.

QUESTIONS:

1. How many areas were you able to check off in the table above? _____

2. How do you define character?

   _____

   _____

3. Why is it important to be a person of character?

   _____

   _____

4. Do you consider yourself to be trustworthy? _____

KNOWLEDGE IS POWER

"I wish I had known that education is the key. That knowledge is power. Now I pick up books and watch educational shows with my husband. I'm seeing how knowledge can elevate you."

- Mary J. Blige

By renewing your mind through reading and learning new things, you can open up a world that you never knew existed. You can become very powerful by becoming a reader. The person with the knowledge has the power. Books are considered vital tools in your personal SUCCESS TOOLBOX.

At a minimum, the books below should be on your bookshelf at all times for quick access, in the mean time you can find some audio titles on YouTube for free:

Table 4-3

1. *"The 7 Habits of Highly Effective People,"* Stephen R. Covey	5. *"Rich Dad, Poor Dad,"* Robert Kiyosaki
2. *"Think and Grow Rich,"* Napoleon Hill	6. *"The 5 Love Languages,"* Gary Chapman
3. *"As a Man Thinketh,"* James Allen	7. *"The 5 Love Languages for Teens,"* Gary Chapman
4. *"Lincoln on Leadership,"* Abraham Lincoln	8. *"The Seven Spiritual Laws of Success,"* Deepak Chopra

Other book recommendations:

_____

_____

_____

STAY MOTIVATED

"In the new economy, information, education, and motivation are everything."

- *William J. Clinton*

Allowing negative people and negative conversations in our lives can be devastating to our personal growth. We must guard ourselves from these people until we are mentally strong enough to tell them that we are not interested in having a conversation if it is not going to be positive. This is not to say that we must run from our problems or stick our heads in the sand and wish it away, but it is about being in a "solution oriented mindset." If we are going to have a negative conversation, then a component of the conversation must be on how to come up with a solution.

Listening to motivational speakers is a way to combat the negative things that our mind may turn to from time to time. If we listen to a positive motivational message every morning before we attend work or school, it can make a major difference in our attitude for the day.

Additionally, as we go through this book and learn how to be successful, we will still have negative thoughts that will enter our minds. You must create a thought interrupter or "change the channel" in your mind. I do this by yelling in my mind (not out loud). When a bad, negative, or sad thought comes to my mind, I simply say, "SHUT UP." My mind will instantly "change the channel" to a different thought.

If shut up is too much for you, simply say "SWITCH" very loud in your mind and think of a time when you did something very silly or saw something very silly done by a pet, child, or adult. Some people use social media as an interrupter. The problem with social media is that it can distract you for too long of a period and can become counterproductive to your work or school day. You want to try this quickly before you allow your thoughts to move you emotionally to anger, sadness, guilt, hurt, or fear. Give it a try, it may actually work for you as well.

Recommended motivational speakers for personal growth and development (Found on YouTube):

Table 4-4

	Les Brown
	Eric Thomas
	T. D. Jakes
	Joel Osteen
	Tony Robbins

Remember, we must renew our minds DAILY. This will require you to change your daily schedule. It is worth every minute of it if you want to live an exceptional life.

Other recommended Speakers:

_____

_____

_____

_____

FORMAL EDUCATION

"Education is the foundation upon which we build our future."
- Christine Gregoire

Many young, and some old, feel as though college is hard to accomplish and some even say that it is not for everyone. College is simply an extension of high school without the supervision of parents and teachers. College work is not hard, but it requires focus, commitment, and the ability to organize your time, your activities, and your life. If you can get through high school, then you are smart enough to get through college. Some young people don't attend college because they can't afford it, or they have to get a job because of their responsibilities (i.e., spouse, kids, sick parent, etc.). There are all sorts of scholarships, loans, and military college funds to help you pay for your higher education.

I suggest that all high school students consider auditing a college class. This is where you make a request through the college to sit in one of their specific classes to see if you would be interested in taking the course. You will find that the material is not difficult, and it will give a since of ease as you prepare for life after high school.

People who start college and leave within 2 years usually fall within these categories:

1. Too much partying without parental supervision
2. Laziness
3. Overtaken by stress
4. Inability to prioritize
5. Pregnancy
6. Finances
7. Personal illness or illness/death of a family member

The first five can be traced back to emotional wellness which leads to academic struggles.

Table 4-5

Associates Degree	Two-year (30 credit-hours): course of study from a junior college, technical college, vocational college or university. Some Associate of Arts (AA) or Associates of Science (AS) degrees are focused on specific subject areas and some are general studies in preparation for a bachelor's degree. *Average 2016 salary = $45K*

Bachelor's Degree	Four or five-year (60+ credit-hours): Undergraduate course of study from a college or university. Bachelor of Arts (B.A.) and Bachelor of Science (B.S.) *Average 2016 salary = $70K*
Master's Degree	Two-Year (40 credit-hours): Graduate course of study from a college or university. Graduates possess advanced knowledge of a specialized body of applied and theoretical topics. *Average 2016 salary = $100K (part-time college instructors add $40K)*
Doctoral Degree	Four – eight years (60-120 semester hours): The Doctorate degree is the most advanced degree you can earn, symbolizing that you have mastered a specific area of study or field of profession. *Average 2016 salary = $140K+ (part-time college professors add $70K)*

QUESTIONS:

1. Do you have a mentor?   Yes | No | I'm Looking for One

2. Do you think that it is OK to have multiple mentors?   Yes | No | Maybe

3. Who is responsible for your SUCCESS in high school, college and in life?

	My teachers		Law enforcement officers
	My parents		The mayor
	My siblings		The economy (i.e., more jobs)
	My significant other		I AM!
	The government (i.e., free grants, welfare, etc.)		The President

4. Who has the power to derail your success and stop you from achieving your goals?

	My teachers		Law enforcement officers
	My parents		The mayor
	My siblings		The economy (i.e., more jobs)
	My significant other		I DO!
	The government (i.e., free grants, welfare, etc.)		The President

5. Have you toured any colleges as a potential student?   YES | NO
   If Yes, which ones? _____

   _____

   Note: College visits can start as early as ten-years-old. There are many city-wide programs that can take you on a college tour for free. Ask your school's counselor for assistance.

6. Which College do you plan to attend?   _____

TECHNICAL SCHOOLS AND CERTIFICATION PROGRAMS

"A high school diploma will no longer be sufficient. But that post-secondary education does not have to be a four-year university or a four-year college. It can be career technical education, vocational education, community college."

- Raja Krishnamoorthi

Job Corps (www.JobCorps.gov)

Job Corps is the largest FREE residential education (you live on campus) and job training program in America for young adults between the ages of 16-24. It is a federally-funded program providing academic and career skills training. There are 119 centers around the nation and in Puerto Rico.

If you have not finished high school, the Job Corps offers GED and High School Diploma courses, prior to entering a trade.

Below you will find the career areas that encompass 81 different trades available:

Table 4-6

Advanced Manufacturing	Auto Repair	Construction
Finance and Business	Healthcare	Homeland Security
Hospitality	Information Technology	Renewal Energy
Retail Sales & Services	Transportation	

Technical Colleges

Each city usually has a local technical school/college that offer certifications in various fields. The careers listed below do not require a 4-year bachelor's degree but may require a 2-year associates degree to go along with the certification. Technical schools may focus on the following technical certifications:

Table 4-7

Truck Driving ($50K)	IT Security ($60K)	Construction ($35K)
Computer Tech ($40K)	II Network Engineer ($65K)	IT Systems Admin ($50K)
Graphic Design ($30K)	Healthcare ($25K)	Finance ($35K)
Project Management ($60K)	Cosmetology/Barbering ($30K year 1, $75K year 5)	General Contractor ($60K)
Process Engineering ($80K)	Commercial Pilot ($60K)	Heating and A/C ($50K)
Certified Insurance Agent ($65K year 1, $200K year 5)	Financial Advisor ($70K year 1, $500K year 5)	Real Estate ($50K year 1, $300K year 5)

*Note: The salaries listed above are **estimates.** Your actual salary will depend on your commitment and dedication to learning your craft and being the best at it. Do your own research to determine the high-end of the salary range. You should expect to hit the high-end once you establish yourself as a professional in the industry.*

These certification courses may be as little as 5-days and others as long as 18 months.

Career Choices That May Not Require a Certification or a Degree[02]

Below is a list of careers that pay well and the organizations will provide on-the-job training:

Table 4-8

Logistics Manager ($80K)	Postal Worker ($52K)	Property Manager ($53K)
Paralegal ($54K)	Locomotive Engineer ($55K)	Transit Police ($56K)
Petroleum Pump Systems Operator ($60K)	Construction Supervisor ($62K)	Mechanic Supervisor ($61K)
Underwater Welder ($60K)	License Inspector ($65K)	

*Note: The salaries listed above are **estimates.** Do your own research for salaries in your area.*

Highest Paid Careers with a Bachelor's, Master's, and/or Doctoral Degree

Medical (Doctoral or Professional Degree)[03]

Table 4-9

Physicians ($208K)	Anesthesiologists ($350K)	Pharmacists ($122K)
Physical Therapists ($85K)	Veterinarian ($88K)	Dentists ($160K)

Nursing (Bachelor's, Master's Degree, or Professional Degree) [04]

Table 4-10

Nurse Anesthetists ($120K)	Nurse Midwives ($105K)	Nurse Practitioners ($107K)
Physicians Assistants ($110K)	Registered Nurse ($60K)	Pain Management Nurse ($90K)

Engineering (Bachelor's Degree)[05]

Table 4-11

Biomedical Engineer ($92K)	Chemical Engineer ($80K)	Civil Engineer ($88K)
Petroleum Engineer ($75K year 1, $190K yr 10)	Electrical Engineer ($60K)	Computer Hardware Eng. ($65K year 1, $100K year 5)
Aerospace Engineer ($65K year 1, $105K year 5)	Architectural Engineer ($100K)	Electrical Engineer ($80K)
Electronic Engineer ($100K)	Software Engineer ($80K)	Industrial Engineer ($65K)
Mechanical Engineer ($70K)	Nuclear Engineer ($75K)	

Legal (Law Degree) [06]

Table 4-12

Trial Lawyers ($140K)	Intellectual Property ($150K)	Tax Attorney ($100K)
Labor ($95K)	Real Estate (85K)	Law School Dean ($400K)
Law Firm Administrator (Bachelor's Degree) - $350K		

Math[02]

Table 4-13

Statistician ($65K)	Physicists ($65K)	Actuarial Math ($75K)
Applied Mathematics ($65K)	Mathematician ($60K)	Financial Accounting ($60K)

Sciences[02]

Table 4-14

Molecular Biologists ($50K)	Chemists ($60K)	Geologists ($65K)
Political Science ($45K)	Food Science ($50K)	

Gaming (Bachelor's and Master's Degree) [07]

Table 4-15

Game Producer ($75K)	Game Programmer ($62K)	Software Engineer ($85K)
Sound Designer ($50K)	Game Designer ($60K)	Artists and Animators ($65K)

School Principals

Table 4-16

Public Schools ($70K)	Charter Schools ($65K)	Private Schools ($200K+)

Other Careers[02]

Table 4-17

Computer Information Systems ($60K)	Construction Management ($62K)	Supply Chain Management ($60K)
Hotel Management ($45K)	International Business ($65K)	Marketing Management ($60K)
Fashion Designer ($45K)		

THE ACTIVE DUTY MILITARY OPTION:

"I admire the military. I guess in a world of villains and heroes, they're my heroes. Their dedication, their commitment, their discipline, their code of ethics."

- *John Cena*

Army, Navy, Air Force, Marine Corps, and Coast Guard

The military can be a great way of life for many people. I personally served 29 years, while I have friends and family members who only served three or four years. The military is a great place to start your professional career. You will be taught a technical skill that you can use in your civilian career but you will learn other things that you can't put a price on like honor, discipline, commitment, dedication, ethics, selflessness, empathy, leadership, and you will develop a strong sense of character.

Here's how it works:

You must visit with your local recruiter. You will be administered the ASVAB test for enlisted personnel. Once you pass the test with a qualifying score, you will get a full physical. After the physical you will be sworn in and placed in the Delayed Entry Program (DEP). The DEP may be 1-24 months, depending on the job you picked.

You are shipped to basic training which can last 2-3 months and technical training for an additional 2-18 months. Each branch of the military has at least 60 careers to choose from. Below you will find a sample of some career choices available:

Enlisted Careers (High School Diploma):

Table 4-18

Medical Technician	Human Resources	Computers
Air Traffic Control	Jet Mechanic	Special Forces
Information Technology	Paralegal	Police
Fire	Logistics	Food services
Administration	Flight Crew	Public affairs
Construction	Pharmacy Technician	Hotel Management
Food Service	Physical Therapy Technician	Dental Technician

Benefits: Pride, accomplishment, housing, food, clothing, world travel, networking, community, lifelong friendships, education, medical benefits

Enlisted Pay[08]:

E-3 under 2 years = *$22K* single person, free meals, free dorms, free uniforms
E-3 under 2 years = *$40K* married (housing and meal allowance included)

Requirements:

U.S. Citizen or resident alien between 17 and 28 years old, physically fit, no credit or good credit, clean criminal record, no record of mental health issues, pass the ASVAB exam, high school diploma (GED allowed for certain careers with a higher than normal ASVAB score).

Officer Careers (Bachelor's Degree):

Table 4-19

Nursing	Engineering	Information Technology
Pilots	Air Traffic Control	Special Forces
Finance	Pilot	Lawyer
Physicians	Dentists	Veterinarian
Public Affairs	Finance/Accounting	Biologists
Pharmacists	Cyber Security	

Officer Pay[08]:

O-1 under 2 years = *$52K* single, *$53K* married
O-3 over 4 years = *$82K* single, *$83K* married

Requirements:

U.S. Citizen or resident alien between 20 and 34 years old, physically fit, good credit, clean criminal record, no record of mental health issues, pass the Armed Forces Officer Qualification Test (AFOQT), Bachelor's Degree from a regionally accredited college or university.

Three ways to commission from civilian to officer in the U.S. military:

1. College Reserve Officers Training Corps (ROTC) - Air Force ROTC, Army ROTC, or Navy ROTC (graduates of Navy ROTC are given a choice to commission in the Marine Corps or Coast Guard)

2. Service Academy

   Army - U.S. Military Academy (West Point, NY)

   Navy – U.S. Naval Academy (Annapolis, MD)

   Air Force – U.S. Air Force Academy (Colorado Springs, CO)

   Coast Guard – U.S. Coast Guard Academy (New London, CT)

   Merchant Marine – U.S. Merchant Marine Academy (Kings Point, NY)

3. Air Force Officer Training School (OTS), Army Officer Candidate School (OCS), Navy OCS, Marine Corps OCS, and Coast Guard OTS

THE RESERVE/NATIONAL GUARD (PART-TIME) MILITARY OPTION:

"The National Guard has served America as both a wartime force and the first military responders in times of domestic crisis. Hundreds of times each year, the nation's governors call upon their Guard troops to respond to fires, floods, hurricanes and other natural disasters."

- Russel Honore

Army Reserve, Navy Reserve, Air Force Reserve, Marine Corps Reserve, Air National Guard and Army National Guard

Reserve and National Guard members attend basic training (2-3 months) and technical training (2-18 additional months) alongside their active duty counterparts. While active duty members are transferred to their duty stations around the world (Germany, Japan, Hawaii, California, etc.), reservists return to their home of record so that they may continue in college and/or their civilian jobs after technical training.

Reserve/Guard members must report from their home of record to their duty station for weekend drill at least 2 days per month, usually on the first weekend of the month. During weekend duty, the members will perform the duty that they were trained to do when they attended technical training. Additionally, Reserve/Guard members are required to spend 15 days during the summer for annual training. Many times, the annual training is performed at other stateside locations as well as locations around the world.

Reservists/Guard members (Enlisted and Officers) have the same career choices as active duty.

A Reserve/Guard member may be away from home during the initial stages of training (boot camp and technical training) for 120 - 600 days depending on the length of their technical training. Recruits who have children may not enter active duty if they are single or divorced. You can, however, become Reserve/Guard members. Contact an active duty recruiter for exceptions to this policy.

National Guard Members Only: Since the national guard is controlled by the Governor and the Governor controls the state schools, some Governors will allow members of the National Guard to attend their state schools for free. For members in Florida, they can attend University of Florida, Florida State University, Florida A&M University, University of South Florida, University of Central Florida, etc. for absolutely free, at the time of writing this book. Each state governor has the right to change that policy at any time.

Caution: Forty-percent of Reserve/Guard recruits change their minds after basic training and make requests to change their status from Reserve or Guard to active duty. This request will NOT be granted, so choose your status wisely. The reason for the request is that Reserve/Guard members were unsure if they would like the military. After basic training graduation, they realize how much they love the military tradition, honor, and dignity that goes with military service. Additionally, their active duty counterparts are bragging about their first duty station in Germany, Hawaii, or England.

Army National Guard SPLIT OPTION:

The Army National Guard will allow incoming high school seniors to attend basic training during the summer prior to their senior year. After graduating basic training, they return to high school. They are required to attend drill weekend once per month during the school year. After graduation, they will immediately attend technical training. After technical training they return home to attend college and/or find a civilian job.

COLLEGE PREPARATION

As you begin to think and talk about college (as early as 8th grade), it is important to start your research so that you are well equipped to make the right decisions and to understand the necessary requirements for entry. Preparation for college entry takes time, focus, and dedication to ensure you are meeting or have met all requirements. Be sure to get your college checklist from your high school guidance counselor as soon as possible and be sure to create a professional relationship with your counselor. Additionally, many teenagers take the SAT/ACT exams as early as 8th or 9th grade.

College Choice

1. Which college or university would like to attend?

You must choose a college, even if you change your mind later.

_____

2. Is this a public or a private college/university? _____

(Private colleges/universities are much more expensive than public schools)

3. Do a Google® Search to find the website of your future college.

4. Go to the MAJORS page and choose a Program of Study (i.e. engineering, music, medicine, etc.):

College of _____ (i.e. Engineering, Music, Education, Medicine, etc.)

Major _____ (i.e. Chemical, Civil, Mechanical Engineer, etc.)

5. Go to the ADMISSIONS page of your favorite college and find the following information:

Average Grade Point Average (GPA)

for previously accepted Freshman: _____ (3.2 – 4.3)

Required SAT Exam Score: _____ (1200 – 1400)

Required ACT Exam Score: _____ (22-32)

Number of High School Courses/Units required for college entry since 9th grade:

English _____ (2-6)

Math _____ (2-6)

Natural Sciences _____ (2-6)

Social Sciences _____ (2-6)

Foreign Language _____ (2-6)

Undergraduate Fees

Cost per credit hour (In-State): $_____ ($100 - $500)

Cost per credit hour (Out-of-State): $_____ ($300 - $900)

Most courses are 3 credit hours. Students average 4-5 courses per semester (10 courses per year or 30 credit hours per year). There are three semesters at most public residential universities (Fall, Spring, and Summer).

 # credit hours to complete first year of your Major: _____ (30-40 hours)

Annual College Costs

Multiply (Cost Per Credit Hour) X (# first year credit hours) = _____ ($10,000)

Annual meal plan: $_____ ($4,000)

Annual housing costs: $_____ ($7,000)

Annual Book costs: Costs vary. Estimated cost is $2,000 per year

Using the sample numbers above, your first year at a public college as an in-state resident may cost $23,000 per year (2018 estimates).

How Can You Afford College?

You can get money from parents, scholarships, student loans, grants, etc. The better the grades you make in high school, the better opportunity you will have to get a scholarship.

Below are some of the top scholarship websites:

www.fastweb.com   www.collegeboard.org   www.Niche.com

www.scholarships.com   www.moolahspot.com   www.collegeNET.com

If it will cost you $23K per year to attend college, you should apply for 10 times that amount in college scholarships ($230K plus). If you have a strong high school GPA (3.5 or higher), you may be offered a scholarship directly from your college/university during enrollment. Also, the higher the GPA, the better dorms you may get to reside in.

Remember to make good choices and do well on all of your classroom exams while in high school because it can determine how much money you get for college and it can determine if you reside in a nicer dorm room.

6. Do a Google® Search to find 10 Great Ways to Win a College Scholarship and list those ways below:

1) _____

2) _____

3) _____

4) _____

5) _____

6) _____

7) _____

8) _____

9) _____

10) _____

Did you know?

Are you aware that when you are awarded multiple scholarships and those scholarships are more than your tuition costs, that your college/university will issue you a refund check at the end of the semester. Some college students have gotten checks for over $20K because their college bills were paid and $20K was the overpayment. In other words, it pays to apply for as many scholarships as possible.

Many scholarships require you to volunteer in your community. Volunteering is the quickest way for people to recognize that you are self-less and that you believe in building stronger communities.

Volunteer Opportunities for Teens and Adults:

Table 4-20

	Read to elementary school kids		Feed the homeless
	Tutor elementary school kids		Work w/babies at local hospitals
	Volunteer at your church		School/community clean-up
	Read to Senior citizens and plan fun activities		Create a youth sports camp (after school or during summer)
	Youth motivational speaker (no drugs, work hard, listen to parents)		

How many hours do you plan to volunteer, each year, while in high school? _____

The more hours that you volunteer, the more likely you will be admitted to a top college/university (granted you have the grades and SAT/ACT scores). They look at the whole-person concept.

College Essay

When applying to a college or university, your application, which includes your high school transcripts, will likely require you to submit a college application essay. Your essay requirements will be 250-600 words. The admissions officer will review hundreds of applications each day and catching their attention with your essay will be important. Many colleges participate in the Common Application System where one application can go to many colleges. With that said, you may only need to write one or two essays.

Common Elements to Use in an Essay:

Table 4-21

	Background		Identity		Interests		Talent
	Hero		Challenges		Setbacks		Overseas travel
	Future goals		Inspiration		Great book		Strong family
	High achiever		Personal growth		# of books read		Leadership
	Love for community		Lessons from volunteering		High School club memberships		Community club memberships
	multiple high schools		Extracurricular activity		Hard working parents		Who do you admire?
	Sports		Military family				

Overcoming Adversity:

Table 4-22

	Adoption		Loss of a friend		Loss of a family member		Raised in economic distress
	Absent parent		Disability		Rejection (bullying)		Homelessness/shelters
	Trauma/abuse		Sick parent		Care-giver		

(Check all that apply above, then as you write, decide if you want to include any of your choices.)

1. Share your story from the heart. Do not brag or talk about how great you are.

2. What did you learn? It is important to find **_positive_** things you have learned through all of the negative things that have happened in life. There is always something to learn, even if it is that you are a "survivor".

3. Never complain or blame others. Remember, you survived your past and you will survive your future.

4. Solve a problem. If you figured out how to become a better person, write down the steps to your journey. You can use the elements throughout this book to show your journey.

5. What captivates you? You can talk about your interests (i.e. math, science, discovery of new concepts, aeronautics, music, dance, military service, reading, literature, business, medicine, etc.).

Let's get started on writing your essay:

_____

_____

_____

_____

_____

_____

_____

_____

_____

_____

_____

_____

_____

_____

_____

_____

_____

_____

_____

Let's get started in the 9th grade developing a strong GPA, excellent ACT/SAT scores, volunteer hours, volunteer activities, compelling college essay, team sports, clubs and leadership activities (i.e. JROTC, AVID, etc.).

QUESTIONS:

1. Are you attending college after high school graduation? If you have already graduated from high school, did you finish college or do you plan to attend?

   _____

   _____

2. If you can't afford college, is the military an option?
   YES | NO | MAYBE

   Note: Seventy-percent (70%) of young people at military boot camp stated that the number one reason they joined the military was to help pay for college?

   _____

   _____

3. How far do you want to go with your education?

   _____

   _____

I was inspired recently when I met a 64-year-old grandmother who is working on her Bachelor's degree in Psychology. It is never too late to develop yourself and to live your dreams.

SPIRITUAL REFERENCE:

"The heart of the prudent acquires knowledge, And the ear of the wise seeks knowledge."
- **Proverbs 18:15 (NKJV)**

FAMOUS QUOTE:

"Education is the most powerful weapon which you can use to change the world."
- **Nelson Mandela**

TAKEAWAYS:

1. There are many paths to success. Pick One!

2. Education is the key to knowledge, wisdom, and success.

AFFIRMATIONS: *(Recite each morning)*

1. I am educated and full of wisdom.
2. I will be accepted into _____ University.

TIME TO SOAR:

Exercise 1: CAREER CHOICES

Materials needed: Pen and smartphone

1. If you were guaranteed success in any career field, what career field would you choose if I paid you $400,000 per year to do it?

   _____

2. How much do people who are currently in your chosen career field make per year with 5 years of experience? Go to www.glassdoor.com to view their salary survey.

   $ _____

After 5 years of experience in your chosen field, you could very well find a business partner who would be interested in helping you start your own business in the same field. After a few years as an entrepreneur and a lot of hard work, you can pay yourself a salary of $400,000 per year.

Chapter 5

WHAT IS STUNTING OUR GROWTH

"I have had fear in the past, yes. I've learned to fight it. But I still have my moments. I just have to remind myself that fear is all within your mind, and that you're only holding yourself back when you give in to it. Even fear of success can be scary."

- *Christina Milian*

The Fear Barrier

Fear was designed to help us when we encounter a bear in the woods and we have to fight the bear, run, or simply freeze from fear (fight, flight, or freeze). It was not designed for long-term use (constant physical, verbal, or sexual abuse in the home, at school, in your neighborhood, or at work) because it has such a negative effect in our bodies. Fear is expressed in your body through anxiety. Suppressing anxiety can turn into depression (deep sadness and worry) and depression can cause all kinds of diseases in your body.

The list below is just a few diseases that **CAN** come from high levels of anxiety that usually stems from childhood hurts, pain, or trauma, as you later approach your 30s, 40s, and 50s:

Table 5-1

Migraines	Cancer
Fibromyalgia	Stroke
Heart disease	Hepatitis
High blood pressure	Chronic Headaches
Irritable bowel syndrome	Diabetes
Hypertension	

Instead of suppressing your anxiety, allow your anxiety to be released by forgiving others (spouse, parents, uncle, aunt, siblings, cousins, supervisors, friends, etc.). Prayer and meditation are strong counteractions to stress and anxiety. Additionally, one of the fastest ways to release fear and anxiety in your life is through Neurolinguistics Programming (NLP) and Time Line Therapy®[01]. Researching NLP is well worth your time.

Here is a list of bad emotions that may feed your fear:

Table 5-2

Sadness	Depression
Anger	Boredom
Guilt	Annoyance
Resentment	Worry
Hate	Criticism
Revenge	Blame

Whatever you are thinking and feeling today is creating your future.

What if you could replace the feelings above with new feelings? The list below are good emotions:

Table 5-3

Love	Gratitude
Joy	Passion
Happiness	Excitement
Joyful Expectation	Hope
Satisfaction	Desire

When a negative event happens in your life or when someone says something to you that is very disappointing, ask yourself two questions.

1) Am I choosing to exhibit LOVE?
2) Am I choosing to exhibit HATE and FEAR?

CHOOSE LOVE, CHOOSE LOVE, CHOOSE LOVE every time and watch your situation change immediately. Darkness can't be removed with darkness. We must turn on our light through LOVE, JOY, and HAPPINESS then watch the darkness leave the room and the light takes over.

I know it may be hard to believe for some people, but we have TOTAL control of our feelings. We can choose negative/bad emotions or we can choose positive/good emotions.

Fear of Failure / Fear of Success

As we strive to be more successful in life, strong belief, unbelievable faith, and massive action will determine how far we will go in life. We must also study and develop ourselves DAILY so that we can develop a strong belief system outside of the belief system that we were taught as a child. Many times, we look at successful people and celebrate their success and say that they are somehow luckier, smarter, more focused, attended a better high school or college, or they may have had a better upbringing than us. The fact of the matter is that they have a stronger belief in themselves, they have learned how to take action and not blame others for their failures, and they are more balanced emotionally.

You have the same capability as other successful people. You have to believe in yourself and your ability to achieve your goals and dreams.

1. Have you ever dreamed about doing something incredible with your life? Probably.
2. Have you ever dreamed about doing something that no one else has ever done? Probably.
3. Do you think that everyone in the world has the EXACT same dream with the exact same clarity that you had? Probably NOT!!

If you were given a specific dream, then it is up to YOU to ensure that the dream is realized. Don't let others tell you that your ideas are crazy or unachievable. They can't see it and don't understand it because it was not a dream that was given to them to birth, but to you. How long will it take to birth your dream? How long does it take for a baby to walk? No one knows, but we never tell the child to sit down and stop trying. The only reason we have patience with babies attempting to walk is because we have seen it work time after time, so we believe that if they just keep trying, they will one-day start walking. I have seen committed action-filled entrepreneurs try time after time to make their business work and if they don't quit, they will see success and sometimes they will see massive success.

Some people also have a fear of success. They may be right at the edge of success and quit. Some people fear success because the idea of making $80,000 or $150,000 per month scares them.

They repeat the following questions in their mind over and over:

Table 5-4

	What if I change when I become wealthy and lose my close friends?
	Can I handle the responsibility of my staff depending on my success to pay their mortgage?
	Can I handle that kind of money, what would I do with it?
	What if I earned $150,000 per month, then lose it all?
	What will I do when family and friends ask me for money?
	Will people like me or just my money?
	What if I make so much money and work too hard and I don't have time for my family?
	What if I become an evil person when I get all of this money? They say that the love of money is the root of all evil.

Choose one above that you believe may hold you back from success

These types of thoughts will keep you poor, scared, or it will ensure you live a very safe and restricted life. The only reason that people make $60,000 per year is because no one has ever taught them how to make $60,000 per month.

Trauma

Unfortunately, physical violence, verbal abuse, inappropriate touching, fondling, inappropriate exposure of body parts, rape, molestation, incest, etc. are activities that are going on daily in communities around our nation, but no one is talking about it. Although it continues to destroy the inner-city community of all races at an alarming rate, African-American children have almost twice the risk of sexual abuse than white children. Children of Hispanic ethnicity have a slightly greater risk than non-Hispanic white children. Of children who are sexually abused, 20% are abused before the age of eight.[02] This secret destroys families and communities everywhere, no matter their socio-economic background. It is a secret parasite that is destroying our children, hampering their social maturity, and stealing their innocence and their ability to create a healthy love and appreciation for authority. It is probably the deepest pain or hurt that any child will experience.

Below is a list of common actions of a person who has been violated sexually:

Table 5-5

	Lash out at loved ones.	Develop extreme anger issues.
	Develop trust issues with authority (parents, teachers, coaches, pastors, law enforcement, military leaders, etc.).	Trigger constant outbursts in school that disrupts an entire classroom (yelling, throwing desks, fighting, etc.)
	Take medications for depression.	Allow certain words to trigger their anger or their extreme outbursts.
	Publicly disrespect the one who is secretly violating them.	Retreat from life and lock themselves in their rooms.
	Develop an addiction to drugs and alcohol and becoming more aggressive when they drink.	Desire professions that are not appropriate (nude dancing, prostitution, porn industry, etc.).
	Develop bi-polar disorder	Cry a lot in public or private.
	Develop a pornography addiction.	Get married at 18 to escape the perpetrator in their home or community
	Fall into a deep depression.	Develop thoughts of suicide.
	Chooses to have a child in middle/high school	Develop an addiction to food.
	Become abnormally anxious about their health, thinking that they suffer from illnesses and diseases (hypochondriac). which may cause them to actually manifest the disease in their bodies.	Develop an unhealthy addiction to material things (i.e. fancy cars, designer clothes, etc.) in an attempt to cover their real pain.
	Difficulty maintaining healthy romantic relationships with one person.	Three or more children from multiple fathers before 25th birthday

The inability to control one's anger due to trauma has led to athletes being suspended or fired from their professional sports teams for battery charges, gun violations, drug violations, etc., causing them to lose millions of dollars. For this very same reason, boys and young men are being kicked off their high school and/or college football teams, getting arrested for fighting and drugs, being kicked out of the house for disrespecting parents, etc. Girls do not escape the consequences of not being able to control their anger, they too are being kicked out of school, they run away from home, become sexually active, and/or they lash out at their boyfriends, friends, and parents and are also getting arrested for fights and drugs.

If we were truly ever able to find out why young people commit suicide, I would venture to say that one-third of suicides by young people (outside of military service/deployments) can be traced back to inappropriate touching, molestation, rape, etc. This is my professional opinion based on thousands of conversations on this subject, but below are the FACTS:

> Children who are sexually abused are at significantly greater risk for later post-traumatic stress (PTSD) and other anxiety symptoms, depression, and suicide attempts. Behavioral problems, including physical aggression, non-compliance, and oppositionality occur frequently among sexually abused children and adolescents.[03]

> Males who are sexually abused are more likely than their non-abused peers to impregnate a teen. In fact, several studies indicate that the sexual abuse of boys is a stronger risk factor for teen pregnancy than the sexual abuse of girls.[04] Among male survivors, more than 70% seek emotional treatment for issues such as substance abuse, suicidal thoughts and attempted suicide.[05] Male sexual abuse survivors have twice the HIV-infection rate of non-abused males. In a study of HIV infected 12 to 20-year-olds, 41% reported a sexual abuse history.[06]

This situation constitutes a family and community emergency because it causes the child to spiral out of control very quickly, causing emotional or physical harm to themselves, their family, or to their classmates.

If this has happened to you, the key is not to blame yourself. It was not your fault. You were not strong enough mentally or physically to fight that person off, ~~of you~~ or to stop the activity from happening. It is also normal for some people to still want love, acceptance, and attention from a family member who violated them, especially if they are a biological relative (father, uncle, aunt, cousin, sibling, etc.). If someone is touching you inappropriately, then they were probably touched when they were younger and are repeating what they've experienced. Some people may even think that molestation is normal because they experienced it for many, many years as a child.

I recently acquired an 11-year-old client who was molested by his mom's boyfriend's sons when he was just 8-years-old and the boys were 10 and 11-years-old. He exhibited issues where he would be calm one moment, then just get angry very quickly, especially when he didn't get his way. He was known to pull a knife on his mother and walk out of the classroom at school whenever his anger surfaced. He was kicked-out of two public schools as well. When he came to me, I was not told that he had been molested. I was informed of his anger issues toward his mother and that he was acting out in school. This young man was also recently diagnosed with ADHD, Bi-Polar, and mild schizophrenia. He had been prescribed anti-depression medication. We worked on a few NLP techniques. After two weeks of using these techniques we saw less anger outbursts towards his mother, but he was still getting in trouble in school for fighting and disrespecting school leaders. I then politely asked his parents if he was ever touched inappropriately, and I was told *"YES"*! Well, that was a big part to leave out of the equation. The next day we met for a session. I explained to him about how it is very unfortunate, but molestation is more common than we realize. For African-Americans it extends back to slave breeding camps. I explained to him that this secret destroys families. His response was, *"I didn't want anyone to know. I don't know if I am supposed to like boys now. I don't want to like boys, I like girls. I get so angry and all I see is RED when boys at school call me gay, I know they are joking around, but it makes me want to hurt someone."*

I used a technique I learned called Neurolinguistic Programming (NLP) and Time Line Therapy® (Dr. Tad James)[01] where it took 10 minutes to help him find learnings or something positive from this traumatic event. After the 10-minute session, I asked him to forgive the boys and write them a letter of forgiveness. He immediately replied, *"Oh no! I am not forgiving them for what they did to me."* I asked him to trust me. He said OK and pulled out a piece of paper and wrote one letter to the boys. He ended it with "I love myself, I forgive myself, and I forgive you". He read it multiple times, then we took it outside and burned the letter. He then said, *"Wow, that was great. I feel better already. I wish I had done that a long time ago. Thank you so much."*

Now that he is almost out of the hole, it is time to help him mend the relationships with his family members and teachers who he has acted out against in the past. Apologizing to his mother, sisters, aunts, grand-parents, teachers, etc. for all of the drama and pain he has put them through. He must now create new behaviors, norms, and routines of empowerment, spirituality, and lifelong success. He is now being taught how to make right choices from this day forward and was taught ways to allow his mind and his emotions to be controlled only by him and God, and no one else. He still has some growing and maturing to do. He does not like to read and educate himself. We are still taking baby steps, but he is on his way to a stronger future. He has fewer outbursts and he is on his way. He still has to believe it's possible and take ALL recommended actions to fully come out of his emotional hole.

Reporting the Incident

Reporting the incident is a very brave and necessary step on your part. I understand how tough the decision will be, but you don't want them to abuse your younger siblings, cousins, or others in the community. Before reporting the incident, do everything you can to get proof. Since everyone has a cell phone, simply hide the phone and record the incident on video or audio if possible. This maybe illegal in some states, but under these circumstances it will be fine in most cases (check your local laws concerning audio/video taping without the other person's consent). It will definitely prove to your parents that this has been going on and it will minimize the chance of them thinking that you are lying. Remember, it is possible that your parents won't believe you because they have been frustrated with you for acting out and participating in bad behavior. They probably had no idea that you were acting out because of the touching incidents.

SEEK HELP

This type of childhood trauma is major and it will have a major effect on the people in your life that you love the most.

Here are the 5 Most Important Relationships Affected when you don't seek help:

1. **Your Parents**: You may lash out at your parents or just hide in your room, reading and crying. You may create an environment of jealousy as you may feel that you were never truly loved by your mom/dad and that they loved your siblings more than you. Also, if your mom or dad don't respond to the accusations as you expect them to, it can build into a very high level of emotional pain for you. I have personally seen or heard of many different parental responses. Some mothers have responded by kicking the boyfriend or husband out of the house, only later to take him back because she was lonely or he convinced her that he didn't do what was he was accused of doing. Some mothers have gotten a gun and shot the accuser. Some fathers have taken a bat to the head of the molester, then called the police. Although most children don't know what response they are expecting from their parent, they are definitely looking for some type of outrage on the part of their parent and the parent's willingness to protecting them in the future at all costs.

2. **Your Spouse**: Your pain could cause you to lash out at your spouse and/or cause you to become a workaholic in your attempt to become successful, despite your pain. If you work all of the time, you won't spend the necessary time it takes to build a strong marriage. Also, if your spouse touches you similar to your attacker, then that can trigger emotional pain as well. Due to inappropriate touching, some victims can only have sexual relations with their spouse when they are intoxicated with alcohol or drugs. Some men or women find it difficult to have sexual relations

with their spouse altogether, which puts a strain on the marriage. This is a sign that they are in a deep emotional hole.

3. **Your Children**: Someone who was traumatized as a child for any reason must get emotional help quickly. When the victim becomes a parent, it is very possible that they can develop a short-fuse with their children. This can cause punishment that may be overly abusive or borderline child abuse. Additionally, you may become overly cautious with your children, not allowing them to leave the house, yet not explaining why. Some mothers force their daughters to wear tight jeans because they are harder to remove and may frustrate a would-be molester.

4. **Your Best Friend**: You may become overly possessive with your best friend's time. Also, you may get jealous when they spend more time with another friend, or their girlfriend/boyfriend instead of spending time with you. Also, you may get frustrated because you do more for them than they are willing to do for you.

5. **Your Supervisor**: Your supervisor may ask you to step up and give a short-notice presentation and because you are shy, reserved and/or don't like to speak to a crowd, he will find someone else who is willing, like Pete, who always steps up to the challenge when asked. Your supervisor will then consider Pete for the next promotion, although you have been there 5 years longer than Pete and you trained Pete.

The bottom line is that there is too much pain and too many affected relationships to hold this traumatic event in your heart.

YOU CAN GET THROUGH THIS, BUT YOU WILL NEED HELP!

Forgiveness of everyone that has ever hurt you, coupled with counseling provided by a Neurolinguistics Programming Coach and Time Line Therapy ® Coach, will provide you with the fastest way to regain and control your own mind and to stop others and their actions from controlling you and your future. You have to take back your life and take back control, but you are not equipped to do it by yourself. Spiritual development is what will keep you, feed your spirit, and give you the faith to know that a better life is ahead of you and finding your life's purpose will allow you to focus on helping others, helping you to feel fulfilled in your life.

The Blame Game

It is very important that we accept responsibility for what happens to us in life. I admit that there are terrible things that people may do to us, but we have to forgive them, let go, and move on.

Here's a list of the most common people that teenagers and many adults blame:

Table 5-6

	Parents		School
	Step-parents		Supervisor
	Siblings		Professor
	Boyfriend/girlfriend		The economy
	Friends		Politicians
	Teachers		President
	Spouse		Police

Please check any of the above who you have blamed over the past 60 days

Blaming others can actually be a selfish act on your part because "your pain" is almost always derived from something that someone did to you. The only way that the act becomes painful for months or years is if you love or loved the person that caused you pain or if they are an authoritative figure. For example, a parent, sibling, spouse, best friend, supervisor, police, teacher, politician, etc.

"It is not fair" or "it is not my fault" is a common statement we tell ourselves to make us feel better. As long as it is someone else's fault, it is then up to **them** to change. At that point, we have given ourselves permission to sit back and take no action.

Once we begin to accept responsibility for our lives, we then have to change or make a decision to act upon a situation to make it better. That thought can be very scary for some because they don't know what to do when they have to take responsibility for their own lives. Many people who don't feel as though they make great decisions will end up marrying someone that they feel is a good decision maker or is bold enough to actually make the hard decisions. People who are slow in their decision-making process have developed a **fear** of criticism associated with making bad decisions, probably because they equate decision making with rejection by others who previously criticized them. Based on all of the personalities in the world, there is a 100% chance that someone will disagree with a decision you have made and maybe even criticize that decision. You can't allow them to distract you. You should avoid listening to someone who you would NOT trade places with in life, career, or relationship. If you are interested in living a life similar to your mentor's, then listen to the thoughts of your mentor, but consider other opinions as just noise.

Four Personal Pillars of Trust

If you are not great at making decisions for your life, don't BLAME others and expect them to change their decision-making process, find yourself a mentor and develop your *Four Personal Pillars of Trust*. The Four Personal Pillars of Trust are the mentors that you call when life gets scary, you fear losing the ability to provide for yourself or your family (getting fired or laid-off), you get nervous based on a difficult decision you need to make, when everything around you seem to be in disarray, or you have a life emergency that you need to navigate.

Below is a list of possible personal pillars of trust:

Table 5-7

Mom	Mentor
Dad	Supervisor
Step-parent	Spouse/significant other
Uncle/Aunt	Barber/Hairstylist
Grandparent	Mature best friend
Coach	Neighbor
Pastor	Sibling

Our natural go-to people are the ones who are responsible for our birth because they "should" know us better than anyone else.

Your *Four Personal Pillars of Trust* are designed to give you sound advice, not to confuse you even further. If you get sound advice after calling your mother, then your father, then go ahead and finalize your decision and move forward. Just say, "Thanks dad, I like mom's idea a little better." Additionally, some of your personal pillars may just listen to you and as you talk about the issue, you may discover the answer on your own, simply because you are in an "action" mindset in trying to figure out what to do. In other words, a personal pillar may simply become a sounding board.

SPIRITUAL REFERENCE:

"For God has not given us a spirit of fear, but of power and of love and of a sound mind."
- **2 Timothy 1:7 (NKJV)**

FAMOUS QUOTE:

"I think, looking back, there was a lot of fear of success in me. When you are successful, you have to keep it up... it requires you to be responsible..."
- **Carlene Carter**

TAKEAWAYS:

1. Fear of success or fear of failure can derail your future. You have everything inside of you to have enormous success. You must educate yourself.

2. Blaming others for your lack of success is a total waste of time. Whatever happened in the past is now history, it already happened, now what are you going to do about it? Will you TAKE ACTION or stick your head in the sand and cry?

AFFIRMATIONS: *(Recite each morning)*

1. I will live a victorious life.
2. I am responsible for my success and will always take action to make life better me and my family.

TIME TO SOAR:

Exercise 1: FORGIVE EVERYONE

Materials needed: Pen

1. Write down the names of everyone who has ever hurt you in your entire life?

2. Some participants will have a list of three names while others may have ten or more.

_____

_____

_____

_____

_____

_____

_____

_____

_____

_____

_____

_____

_____

Exercise 2: WRITE THEM A LETTER

Materials needed: Notepad and pen

1. It's time to write a letter to EVERYONE you identified in Exercise 1.

2. The letters must have 3 components:

    a. Include all your negative emotions in the letter because this will be the last time these emotions are expressed. Also, write down how you expected this person to treat you at the time of the emotional or physical pain.

    b. Include what you have learned from this situation that is positive (even if the only thing that you learned was that you survived, and that the ordeal made you a stronger person).

        1) Did this event make you a kinder, more empathetic person to your friends, siblings, cousins, etc.?
        2) Did this event make you want to be a better parent?
        3) Did this event make you a hard worker?
        4) Did this event make you want to become more successful?
        5) Did this event make you seek out your life's passion where you are always lending a helping hand to other people?
        6) Did this event bring you closer to God or caused you to study His principles?
        7) Did this event cause you to want to do more with your life?

    c. End each letter with "I love myself, I forgive myself, and I forgive you".

3. If you are 18-years-old or older, I suggest that you read the letter three times, then BURN each letter separately. This can be done in the kitchen sink, on the side with the garbage disposal. If you are a minor, then I suggest that you RIP IT UP into tiny little pieces and flush each letter separately down the toilet. It is important to watch the letter as it disappears into the toilet.

Chapter 6

MANAGE EXPECTATIONS

"I find my life is a lot easier the lower I keep my expectations."
- Bill Watterson

In this chapter, we discuss the expectations a parent has for their teenage children, their adult children, and what teenagers expect from their parents. This is important if you want to meet the expectations of the people who you love and who love you. Many times, our parents, children, spouse, friends, coworkers, and supervisors have unrealistic expectations of us, but never tell us what those expectations are. Since we don't know what is expected, we seem to disappoint people over and over again. Have you ever asked someone what they expect of you and their response was, "Well, you should know" or "I don't have any expectations of you," yet their feelings were hurt, for example, because you chose to visit your girlfriend/boyfriend, instead of spending a second night at the hospital with them when they were sick?

"What are your expectations of me?" is a powerful question for your loved ones, co-workers, and supervisors when they seem to get angry or hurt by your actions. It forces them to be more realistic in their expectations. Employees usually have a long list of expectations in their mind for their leadership at work, but when asked to voice those expectations, the list gets short very quickly because they realize subconsciously that their expectations were unrealistic. For example, someone may expect their supervisor to call them and wake them up when they don't show up to work on time. Yet, they would never voice that in an expectation conversation. When expectations are communicated, it makes for a great relationship. You never have to say, "I wonder if I hurt her feelings?" If you know her expectations, then you know that her feelings were not hurt.

Top 10 List of Things that Parents Expect from their Teenagers:

1. **School:** Stay focused, do your homework, respect your teachers, graduate on time, and start thinking and preparing for college as early as 12-years-old.

2. **Friends/Social Media:** Become a leader and not follower and stay away from bad influences. Don't let social media define who you are. Loving yourself is much more important than "LIKES" on social media

3. **Home:** Keep your room clean and do your chores.

4. **Siblings:** Love and protect your sisters and brothers. Don't be envious and allow your mind to believe that they are favored over you. If you look for them to be favored, you will create that reality in your mind, although it may never actually exist. Parents naturally worry about the child who has had the most emotional issues. This concern may look like favoritism, but it is not. If you have a stronger mindset, if you are more successful in school and complete chores as asked, you may not get as much attention as the child who is struggling with something (i.e. weight, a disability, illness, rejection, trauma, missing a biological mother or father, making friends, etc.). The child who "can't get it together" may appear to be favored but actually your parents are just more concerned about that child's future and may spend extra time trying to support him or her to help them feel normal. Additionally, you may be the child that makes bad decisions and feel as though your parents favor the sibling who is emotionally stronger, makes better grades, who plays sports, and who doesn't get in as much trouble. You may even get upset when your sibling is praised.

5. **Relationships:** Be careful in picking a boyfriend/girlfriend and ensure they are capable of loving and respecting you. Don't date/marry someone just to prove to your parents that you are an adult and are capable of making a relationship work, when it is very obvious that he or she doesn't respect you and you are not good together. Many times, we date people that are in a much deeper emotional hole than ourselves, just so that we can feel needed, wanted, helpful, or so that we can control that person. It is possible that when the patient (boyfriend/girlfriend) gets well (climb out of the emotional hole) that they may "walk out of your care." In other words, we act as though we are the nurse and our significant other is the patient. When that person gets well, then they don't need us anymore because the relationship was built on philia (brotherly) love and their brokenness and not on eros (romantic) love and mutual respect. Financially speaking, in 2017 it takes $70,000 per year minimum in income (in most U.S. cities) for a household to live comfortably (tithe, savings, apartment/small home, 2 car payments, gas, car repairs, insurance, internet/cable, cell phone, electric, water, food for 3, etc.), does

your boyfriend/girlfriend's career support these types of expenses? Will he/she be able to contribute to the household? Some cultures encourage their children to live at home (after college), save $50,000 from their pay over 3 years, then get married, move out, purchase a home, start a family, etc.

6. **Parents:** Respect your mother, father, and/or step-parents even when you don't understand why they made a particular decision. Express your feeling to them without yelling, walking away, or getting emotional.

7. **Attitude:** Keep an attitude of gratitude. Say "Thank you, please, I appreciate that, and May I." Additionally, don't forget to use the tried and true form of respect by saying, "Yes Ma'am and No Sir".

8. **Authority:** Respect everyone who has been put in authority over you. If they disrespect you, contact someone in authority who is able to handle the situation. You may not see the punishment rendered but remember that you have done your part by reporting it, now allow the leaders to do their part. Show respect for the police, military, and the laws of the land.

9. **Self-Expression:** Practice "truth-talk" daily and understand that parents and teachers may already know the answer before they ask you. They just want to see if you will tell the truth. Treat people with kindness, respect, and always tell the truth.

10. **Dream Big:** Most parents want their children to be better and more successful than they are. Every generation should produce smarter, more determined children. Whatever you want to be in life, stay focused, educate yourself, and get mentored so that you can achieve your dreams and goals and live a life worth emulating. Don't ever stop dreaming!!

What do Parents Expect from their ADULT Children?

Top 4 list of things that every parent wants for their **adult** children:

1. **Independence:** Get a skill, find a career, go to college so that you will become independent of your parents and you will be able to pay your own way in life (mortgage/rent, electric, water, car, insurance, cell phone, etc.). If you are sleeping on someone else's couch, you are not independent. Many parents are willing to pay thousands of dollars for your college education because college creates a

skillset and enables higher future earnings potential for you and your family. Many parents would rather pay the high price of a college education than pay your light bill this month, your rent three months from now, and your cell phone bill in four months. If you lack a college education and technical skills, this can lead to poor self-esteem, frustration, stress, low-paying jobs, and lower level living. If you can't afford college/technical school and haven't figured out life yet, the military is a great place to find your footing and will help build self-esteem, lower frustration, provide decent pay that gets better over time, free meals, worldwide travel, worldwide respect, and a medium level of living, all between the ages of 18 and 29-years-old.

2. **Love and Respect:** Find a significant other who loves and respects you. Saying and having feelings of love is easy for most people. Showing the action of love is not so easy. People who you love want you to show them that you love them by doing and not just saying. Respect is also an action. When you respect someone, you are kind, considerate, generous, you choose your words carefully, you honor boundaries, you compromise, you can admit when you are wrong, and you don't allow others to hurt your partner.

3. **Spiritual Life:** Develop a spiritual life, study your religion faithfully, and attend services weekly to help keep your thoughts pure.

4. **Health:** Eat healthy, visit your doctor as necessary, and exercise regularly.

What Do Teenagers Expect from Their Parents?

Top 10 list of things teenagers want from their parents

1. **Unconditional Love:** Children expect unconditional love from the two-people responsible for their birth, no matter if everyone lives in the same household or not. Unconditional love has no conditions and it includes acceptance, patience, and understanding.

   "Mom, do you love me just like I am? I know that I make bad decisions often and that I have a lot of maturing to do, but I still need your love. Many times, it feels as though you only love me when I act a certain way, do something for you or whenever I achieve something that you approve of," said John.

Below are a few examples of conditional love and unconditional love:

Conditional love: If you get good grades, then I will be proud of you.

Unconditional love: I love you and I am so proud of you. What do we need to do to ensure you are getting better grades in school? I know you are capable of more. Do you need a tutor?

Conditional love: Why can't you stop getting in trouble and be more like your sister?

Unconditional love: I love you sweetheart. I know you say that you are not bothered by the fact that your father hardly ever returns your phone calls, so I will try to communicate better with him to help him understand your needs and expectations. But don't give up on your father because he loves you too, but he doesn't always know how to show you.

Conditional love: Your brother made the All-Star Team, so I can't attend your last three soccer games.

Unconditional love: I love you son and I am so proud of you. Now that your brother has made the All-Star team, we need to figure out a new schedule for the family. Can you help me come up with a win-win situation so that everyone is happy? Can you figure out a plan for everyone to be able to make as many games as possible, because I want to be there for ALL of my children.

2. **Pride/Acceptance:**   Children need to know that their parents love them and are proud of them. A child will never tell you to stop saying, "I love you and I'm proud of you." Additionally, when mom or dad attends a child's sporting event, many times that child will play harder than ever before, just so that they can hear, "Great game, I am so proud of you." If a biological parent that lives out of town visits and attends the game, that child will be beaming with pride (no intentional slight against the step-parent/grand-parent who may have taught him/her the game or may even be the coach).

3. **Understanding and Patience:** A teenager deals with so much pressure in middle/high school and they don't quite know how to talk about it because it may be embarrassing to talk about or their issue may seem trivial to most adults. Here are just a few things that may bother teenagers:

Table 6-1

	Bullying, including social media harassment
	Having a tough time making new friends
	Fitting into the school environment and being accepted by teachers and students
	Being laughed at, ridiculed, or embarrassed by an upper-classman or teacher
	Interested in dating someone, but not sure if that person likes them
	Struggles with their sexuality
	Break-up of a friendship or relationship
	Boys/girls sexually harassing each other through unwanted touching, grabbing, and vulgar conversations
	Feeling disliked or misunderstood by teachers
	Having problems reading or comprehending school work, so they just act out instead of speaking up. They could suffer from dyslexia.

By the time the teenager gets home from school, he appears to the parents to be scattered in his thoughts or disinterested in what is going on at home. In actuality, he is looking for peace, love, and understanding when he arrives home after school. Teenagers want to talk about what happened to them that day, but many times mom or dad is too tired or not interested in talking. This is an example of how a two-parent household can help with the balance that children need in life. When one parent is tired or not interested, the teenager can go to the other parent. If there's no one at home who's willing to show love and attention to a teenager, teenagers will begin to look for that love in others, and unfortunately may become entangled in undesirable interactions or relationships, for example, undesirable friends, undesirable romantic relationships, gangs, internet stalkers, older men/women, etc. Whatever the "clan" of friends is doing, the teenager will feel that it is acceptable for him to do as well, for example stealing, drinking, marijuana, cigarettes, vaping, fighting, partying, sex, etc.

Kids who are loved by both biological parents may also experience these things as teenagers if the parents are not watching and correcting the behavior. For instance, if the parents drank alcohol as teenagers, they may be fine with their children trying it as a teenager. Parents must discipline their children and let them know what acceptable behavior is and what it is not, otherwise the child will view deviant behavior as no big deal. If a parent does not respond to bad behavior, it is considered acceptable behavior by the child. A child might say, "My mom knows I smoke weed, but she never says anything, so it's cool".

4. **Discipline**: Teenagers would rather have a loving parent than a parental friend. We all want discipline in our lives, whether we admit it or not. Discipline is defined as the practice of training people to obey rules or a code of behavior, using punishment to correct disobedience. The punishment that is very prevalent today is the taking of the child's cell phone, video game or denying them the opportunity to play sports. Children want equal and fair discipline, but as parents with multiple children know, what works as discipline for one child, may not work for the other. Many children secretly view their parents as weak or as pushovers when they don't deliver on their threatened punishments. They will probably never say it to the parents, but they will say it to their friends. Parents must say what they mean, and they must mean what they say. If you say to them, "If you keep smoking marijuana, I'm going to send you to a drug rehab center," then you must do just that. If you are not going to follow through, don't use the threat.

5. **Encouragement**: Teenagers want their parents to be their biggest cheerleaders and to tell them that they can accomplish anything that they put their minds to. Our job as parents is to encourage our young people to be the best at everything they do, and when they fail, which everyone does, be there to help them, comfort them, and lovingly highlight the learning moment from the failed event.

6. **Time**: Teenagers want their parents to spend time with them. Sometimes, for teenagers who are very busy with school activities and their friends, this may not always seem true. Parents with multiple children should consider having a date night with each individual child at least once per month. It could be as simple as going out for ice cream and talking about something fun that the teenager enjoys. Leave your cell phone in the car...no distractions during their time. Also, parents must understand how important friends are to teenagers. When everything is going well between mom and dad, teenagers are free to explore healthy relationships with their friends. If home life is terrible, then teenagers are way too dependent on their friendships. Their friends are normally not equipped to carry the burden of providing all of the love and attention needed by this child who hates their life at home. They are labeled as "too needy, extra, too dependent, too sensitive, immature, gullible, etc.".

7. **Hugs**: Teenagers want their parents to hug them, even when they pull away. If parents stop hugging their children, the child will wonder if they did something to offend the parent. A hug and kiss to start a child's day, even an adult's day, can go a long way to starting the day off right.

8. **Celebrations**: Teenagers want to be celebrated by their parents. Birthdays, recitals, athletic events, speeches, concerts, etc. are great moments of celebration. Some children prefer that their parents bring special thoughtful gifts to these events to show their love and encourage them to succeed by saying, "You can do it, I believe in you," right before the start of the event. These events will become the most memorable for your child and deserves celebration and not criticism. Something to remember is that people go where they are celebrated, not where they are simply tolerated. Parents should not allow another adult or peer with negative influence to celebrate their child more than they do.

9. **Healthy Communications:** Unfortunately, when a parent does not live with their biological child, that child feels slighted by that parent, especially if that parent is raising other children. I hear about this all of the time with my clients. Fathers and mothers should make a point to have healthy communications with ALL of your children at least *4 times per week*. Don't expect a step-parent, sibling, or your parents to pick up that slack...YOU PICK UP YOUR OWN SLACK. If you don't tell your daughter she is smart, beautiful, intelligent, and a wonderful person, some emotionally unbalanced boy will be happy to do it for you and she will call him "Daddy".

10. **Apology:** If your kids are mad at you and won't return your calls, they are not saying that they don't want you in their lives, they are saying, "TRY HARDER". If you have hurt your child or abandoned them in the past and are ready to make it right, keep calling. Fly into your child's city or college campus and show up at their doorstep to apologize. Tell them that you are not leaving until you make it right. Some parents feel that as the adult, their children should call them, but the child feels as though their parent abandoned them and that they should call them. It becomes a no-win standoff. No one said parenting is easy, but it is worth it.

Questions:

1. Is discipline important? If you were never disciplined and taught right from wrong, do you think that you would choose to do good or bad things in your life?

   _____

   _____

2. If you were in a grocery store and witnessed a 5-year-old running through the store, pulling food from the shelves and scattering the food on the floor, what would be your first question concerning this child?

   _____

   _____

3. Reviewing the "Top Ten" list of things teenagers wants from their parents, what are the top five that you prefer to receive from your parents?

   _____

   _____

   _____

   _____

SPIRITUAL REFERENCE:

"Children, obey your parents in all things, for this is well pleasing to the Lord."
 - **Colossians 3:20 (NKJV)**

FAMOUS QUOTE:

"Blessed is he who expects nothing, for he shall never be disappointed."
- Alexander Pope

TAKEAWAYS:

1. Happiness should be dependent on you and God. The more you expect someone else to make you happy, the more that person will disappoint you. Most people are not aware of how to make themselves happy, so how can you expect them to make you happy.

2. Family, friends, and supervisors have certain expectations of you, whether you know it or not. It is possible for you to continually disappoint them unless you ask them what those expectations are.

3. Most people's expectations of siblings, parents, children, friends, and supervisors are very unrealistic. One does not realize how unrealistic it is until those expectations are verbalized and/or written down.

AFFIRMATIONS: *(Recite each morning)*

1. I am a great communicator.
2. I only have high expectations of myself and I realize others are doing the best they can with what they have.

TIME TO SOAR:

Exercise 1: MANAGE EXPECTATIONS

Materials needed: Pen and phone

1. What are your expectations of family, friends, teachers, and leaders? What can others do or say to make you happy or what can they do or say to make you sad?

   Remember, if you have no expectations, that means that they could NEVER disappoint you.

Mom: _____

_____

_____

_____

_____

Dad: _____

_____

_____

_____

_____

Sister: _____

_____

_____

_____

_____

Brother: _____

_____

_____

_____

_____

Best Friend #1: _____

_____

_____

_____

_____

Best Friend #2: _____

_____

_____

_____

_____

Supervisor/Teacher/Coach: _____

_____

_____

_____

_____

Significant Other_____ ⁄ _____

_____

_____

_____

_____

2. Once you have completed #1 above, call each person and ask them what they expect of you?

You: Hey _____. I have been doing some self-reflection in my life and I want to know if you have any expectations of me as your _____ (child, brother, subordinate, friend, etc.).

Them: Well, I don't think I have ***any*** expectations of you.

You: Then I guess I could ***never*** disappoint you.

Them: Well, when you put it that way, I expect for you to

_____.

You: Thank you for telling me what you expect of me. It will help me ensure that I meet those expectations as much as I can. Now, can I tell you what I expect of you as my (mother, father, sister, brother, aunt, uncle, friend, or leader)?

> *Note: People are not required to meet your expectations, no matter how much you scream and shout. Should you allow that person to define your life and your future or do you take control of your life and your future? The more you depend on another human being to fulfill your happiness, the more you will find yourself disappointed.*

Take control of your life, get focused (like a heat seeking missile moving towards it's target) and if others want to get on board, then fine, but you have a wonderful life to live and you can't let others stop you. Make your family, your community, and your nation proud of you and your accomplishments.

"Formal education will make you a living; self-education will make you a fortune."

- Jim Rohn

Chapter 7

DEVELOP STRONG FINANCES AND GENERATIONAL WEALTH

"I believe that through knowledge and discipline, financial wealth is possible for all of us."

- Dave Ramsey

Unfortunately, the school system does not teach young people how build generational wealth. Generational wealth represents money, real estate, stocks/bonds, businesses, etc. that you leave for your grandchildren's children to inherit. Many young people are taught how to spend, but not how to save their money. According to a Washington Post article on *Wealth Inequality* (2015), 20% of the wealthiest Americans owns 90% of the wealth.

Interestingly enough is that if the top 20% of the wealthiest Americans were to share their wealth with the rest of America and give each person $1 million, within three short years, the monies will be back in the hands of the top 20%. Most poor people have a consumer mentality and will immediately take their $1 million and purchase a home, fancy car, and designer clothes. The top 20% are the ones who owns the mortgage companies, banks, dealerships, and clothing houses/department stores.

The top 20% of the wealthiest Americans have a different mindset and approach to dealing with wealth. They would simply take that same $1 million and *invest* it in real estate, stocks/bonds, bank lending, businesses, etc. to make it grow and then eventually begin to live off of the interest that is generated. They continue to drive their $25,000 car and live in their $200,000 home until they reach the $10 million point.

If you were to start purchasing real estate in your early 20's, instead of a fancy car, then you can start on this lucrative path to generational wealth. The idea is to purchase a property at a great price and renovate that property. After renovation, you rent the property and now the renter is paying off the mortgage for you. Within two years, you purchase another property and do the same thing. By the time you are 45-years-old, you could own 10+ properties worth over $3 million that bring in $20,000 per month in income and $10,000 per month in profit. It is OK to partner with others in this venture on your first few properties, just ensure that a real estate attorney is involved that will clearly layout everyone's responsibilities and their share of the profits.

Here are some tips for creating generational wealth:

1. Millionaire Mentor: If you want to be rich, don't ask poor people for their advice, ask a millionaire to advise you.

2. Read, read, read
   a. Investment books
   b. Stock Market Trading books
   c. Residential and Commercial Real Estate Investing
   d. "Think and Grow Rich" by Napoleon Hill
   e. "As a Man Thinketh" by James Allen
   f. "Rich Dad Poor Dad" by Robert Kiyosaki

3. Hire a financial planner immediately as soon as you start working, no matter how much you make (i.e. Northwestern Mutual®, Edward Jones Financial®, USAA Investments®, etc.). It is important to learn how to manage $35,000 per year so that you will have the knowledge to later manage $400,000 per year.

4. My son Dexter Wyckoff works for Northwestern Mutual ® and suggests the following rule for your income:

20/60/20 RULE

First 20%:

Save and invest the first 20% of your salary. If you make $5,000 per month, you would save $1,000 each month.

- *Emergency Fund Account*: Before you start investing, you should first save 3-6 months of salary for emergencies. It would take 15 months to save $15,000 which would be equal to a 3-month emergency fund.

- *Investing*: Invest 10% or $500 per month into a real-estate fund to purchase homes, invest in a mutual fund, and/or in the stock market.

- *Savings Account*: After you have built an emergency fund, began building up your personal savings account. These monies should be placed in separate accounts.

Second 60%:

Pay your bills with the other 60% of your salary. See the example below using the $5,000 per month example:

- *Tithe/Giving*: $500 (10%)
- *Rent/House Payment and Home Taxes*: $1,250 (25%)
- *Car Payment/Car Insurance/Gas/Repairs*: $500 (10%)
- *Food*: $500 (10%)
- *Utilities*: $200 (4%)
- *Credit Cards*: $50 (1%)

Final 20%:

The final 20% is used as discretionary funds. This money is used for luxuries and anything you wish to spend it on.   See the example below using the $5,000 per month example:

- *Eating Out/Pizza Night*: $200 (4%)
- *Movies and Entertainment: $100 (2%)*
- Cable/Internet: $150 (3%)
- Birthday Gifts/Family Loans: $100 (2%)
- Hair and Nails: $150 (3%)
- Clothes/Shoes: $100 (2%)
- Cell Phone: $100 (2%)
- Healthcare/Toiletries: $50 (1%)
- Life Insurance: $50 (1%)

5. Do research on "The Law of Sowing and Reaping," it is important to give to your church or a charity that you believe in. When you give to others, it will be given back to you in excess.

6. Create a budget using the sample above and don't spend more than you make.

7. Don't allow stuff to control your life (sacrifice your spending habits).

8. Purchase a health plan and life insurance policy for your spouse and children.

9. Save your money and pass it to your grandchildren.

10. Be careful of the "what about me" mindset where you buy what you want and struggle for what you need.

11. Pay cash for everything (i.e. cars, homes, etc.) and stay away from credit card debt. You should only own one credit card. I personally own one personal credit card and one business credit card. When I was 25-years-old, I owned 12 credit cards because the credit card companies kept sending me these pre-approved offers. I would not recommend that today.

A great introduction to investing in stocks and bonds is through a smart phone application called Acorns®. Acorns® will allow you to use your debit card and it will round-up to the nearest dollar for every purchase that you make. If you make a $3.01 purchase, Acorns will take $0.99 and invest it for you. They wait until the end of each day and round-up all of your purchases for the day, then take the money (i.e. $7.82, $6.31, $9.64, etc.) out of your account as if it was a debit card transaction. You can also setup automatic weekly or monthly payments.

Additionally, if the company or organization where you work offers a matching 401K Retirement Plan, I would recommend investing in that first, before looking at other investments. The reason is that the company matches a percentage of the amount of money that you invest. This percentage is usually much higher than if you invested on your own through an application like Acorns ®.

If you invest in your company's 401K Plan, using the $5,000 per month example above you could earn the following:

- Invest 2% or $100 per month, the company will also 2% or $100 per month
- Invest 4% or $200 per month, the company will also invest $200 per month
- Invest 8% or $400 per month, the company will **only** invest $200 per month due to the maximum of 4% matching funds.

Note: The above budget and investment examples are simply hypothetical. You should seek out a financial advisor and speak to the human resource department about matching 401K funds for your organization.

QUESTIONS:

1. Do you have a job? YES | NO

2. Do you have a checking and savings account? YES | NO

3. When you earn income, do you save your money or do you spend it as soon as you get it?

SPIRITUAL REFERENCE:

"Wealth gained by dishonesty will be diminished, but he who gathers by labor will increase"
- **Proverbs 13:11 (NKJV)**

FAMOUS QUOTE:

"Try to save something while your salary is small; it's impossible to save after you begin to earn more."
- **Jack Benny**

TAKEAWAYS:

1. Use the 20/60/20 Rule to create a budget that will put you on the path to saving and investing.

2. Invest in real-estate because it appreciates over time.

3. Invest in the stock market for the long term because history has shown that your net worth will increase.

AFFIRMATIONS: *(Recite each morning)*

1. I am a saver and I am an investor.
2. I will read at least one book on investing once per month.

TIME TO SOAR:

Exercise 1: SPENDING AND SAVING

Materials needed: Smart phone

1. You have been notified that your great uncle passed away and left you $1 million dollars. Over the next 12 months, how will you spend the money?

   Purchase price of your new car: $_____

   Purchase price of your new home: $_____

   Purchase price of your new clothing/shoes: $_____

   Purchase price of your new jewelry: $_____

   Purchase price of technology (i.e. video game console, computer, phone, flat screen TV, etc.): $_____

   Purchase price of travel (i.e. cruise, trips overseas, visiting family, going to theme parks, etc.): $_____

   How much given to parents: $_____

   How much loaned to friends and family: $_____

   How much goes to savings: $_____

   How much goes toward investing: $_____

   TOTAL SPENT YEAR 1: $_____ TOTAL INVESTED/SAVED YEAR 1 $_____

Chapter 8

DEVELOP PERSONAL AND PROFESSIONAL RELATIONSHIPS

"In many ways, effective communication begins with mutual respect, communication that inspires, and encourages others to do their best."

- Zig Ziglar

Many of today's youth are not interested in interacting with adults outside of their family and/or teachers. Most adults will be drawn to young people who can effectively communicate and are involved in their community. It is important for a young person to make an impression with adults who possess possible volunteer opportunities, internships, career, and/or business opportunities for that young person.

5 Ways to Spark Conversation when Meeting Someone for the First Time:

Table 8-1

1. What **_school_** did you attend? Did you attend college locally?

2. What **_city_** did you grow up in? Do you live in the area?

3. What is your **_profession_**? How long have you been doing that?

4. Are you active in the **_community_**?

5. Tell me about your **_family_**? Do you have any brothers and sisters?

When you attend an event where you are representing your high school, college, or your employer, it is very important to move around the room and meet new people. You should spend less than five minutes per person, then you should move on to the next person. Below you will find a good introduction:

You: *Good evening Ma'am. My name is Jason Smith of Florida Technical University.*

Ms. Johnson: *Hello Jason, I am Julia Johnson and it is a pleasure to meet you.*

You: *Likewise, Ma'am. If you don't mind me asking, are you from this area?*

Ms. Johnson: *Yes, Jason, I am from this area. What about you?*

You: *I am actually from Jacksonville, but I've been in the area for about 3 years now. I like it a lot, especially the people. They are very hospitable in this area.*

From that point, the conversation should start to flow. Stay away from religion and politics. After the five minutes are up, simply say, "Mrs. Johnson, it was a pleasure meeting you. Do you have a business card?" After exchanging business cards, excuse yourself, get something to drink, then decide who you will meet next. It also helps if someone is taking you around and introducing you.

Here are some reasons why building a large network is important:

1. Job opportunities
2. Someone may be interested in investing in your project or business
3. Community service opportunities
4. Opportunity to join a private organization or board of directors
5. Opportunity for you to invest in someone else's project (i.e. time or money)
6. Opportunity for others to connect with what you are doing

QUESTIONS:

1. Do your friends tell you that you are a good communicator?
   YES | NO

2. If during a conversation at a formal dinner in college, someone asks you who are you voting for in the next mayoral election, how can you *avoid* giving an answer and getting involved in political conversations?

   _____

   _____

SPIRITUAL REFERENCE:

"Make no friendship with an angry man, And with a furious man do not go."
- **Proverbs 22:24 (NKJV)**

FAMOUS QUOTE:

"I want to keep meeting new people, enlarging my circle of friends. I have great friends now... really good people. But I'm always ready for what comes next."
- **Paula Danziger**

TAKEAWAYS:

1. Meeting new people is an art. Learn it.

2. You never know who you might meet when you are at an event. Be kind to everyone.

AFFIRMATIONS: *(Recite each morning)*

1. I am a great communicator.

TIME TO SOAR:

Exercise 1: NETWORKING INTERVIEW

Materials needed: Pen and notepad

Environment: Classroom partner or local coffee house

1. If you are in a classroom, choose a partner.

2. If you are in a coffee house order a cup of coffee or cup of water. Have a seat. Scan the room to find someone who doesn't look like you who may be sitting and enjoying their coffee or working on their laptop. Approach them and let them know that you are working on a project and if they could spare 4 minutes of their time to answer some questions.

    a. Choose a partner

    b. In the coffee house, it is similar to an interview. In the classroom, you want to have a dialog where you gather information on each other. Use the information below to record the information on the other person:
    Partner's Name: _____

    School Attended/Attending: _____

    College Attended/Plan to Attend: _____

    Number of siblings: _____

    Mom's Occupation: _____

    Dad's Occupation: _____

    Volunteer Activities: _____

    Sports or Clubs: _____

    Tell Me One Thing that Most People Don't Know About You:

    _____

Chapter 9

MANNERS MATTER

"Good manners will open doors that the best education cannot."

- Clarence Thomas

Unfortunately, etiquette is not being stressed with young people today as much as it was prior to the 1990's.

If you are not sure what to say around people who are not of your ethnic background, the easiest thing to remember is that everyone enjoys being treated with dignity and respect. Be nice and you will do fine. You can never go wrong with "Yes Ma'am" and "Yes Sir".

Many times, your college professors, coaches, or work supervisors appear to be very nice and accommodating. Be careful and don't get too comfortable or familiar with people who are decision makers in your life. When you get too comfortable, it hinders your leader's ability to lead you or you may respond to their leadership in a way that is OK in private, but disrespectful in public and around other students, players, or employees. Mind your manners when working for someone else, or when under someone else's leadership. When you start your own organization, you can run it as you please. "Keeping it Real" on your job is not a good quality and it equates to $9 - $13 per-hour, then your pay will likely stop increasing. I have never seen a job description that asks for employees to "keep it real". If you owned a company and your net worth was $30 million dollars, would you pay someone like you or one of your friends $100,000 of your hard-earned money to work at your company? What kind of person would you want to hire. What if the job involves meeting with wealthy clients? Would you hire someone that comes to work angry or sad all of the time, then says, "well, I just keep it real"?

You should always be professional, courteous, and speak to people respectfully. If you are not sure how to treat people in this manner, please go back and read the previous chapters.

Good manners are cost effective. They not only increase the quality of life in the workplace, they contribute to employee morale, embellish the company image, and play a major role in generating profit.

- *Letitia Baldrige*

Profanity, politics, religion, race, and sex (including sexual preferences) should never become a topic with anyone attached to your high school leadership, college leadership, or anyone associated with your employment. These are private conversations that should only take place in the presence of trusted friends and family.

Below you will find some basic courtesies that should be extended by a man and a woman:

Gentlemen

Table 9-1

	Open the door for a lady, (i.e. car door, door at a store, restaurant, or business, etc.)
	Never allow someone else to open the door or hold a door for you to walk in (especially a female), always invite them to go ahead of you as you hold the door for the people coming in behind you. If they insist on holding the door for you, say "thank you" as you walk through.
	Do not sit at the head of the table unless you are the birthday boy, or you are paying everyone's bill.
	Open the car door for the lady when entering the vehicle.
	Get out and open the lady's car door when exiting the vehicle.
	Never use profanity, talk about religion or politics at work – even while at lunch, or at an after-hours event.
	Never allow a lady to carry a box or anything heavy in your presence.
	If you arrive to the door before everyone else, hold the door open for others, up to 30 seconds if necessary (it can make a huge impression on the person and he or she will probably brag about your kindness).
	Always sit facing the door of a restaurant to be alert if something bad or suspicious appears to be happening inside or outside.
	When walking on a sidewalk, always make sure that you are walking closest to the street...just in case you need to push the woman to safety.
	If all of the seats at an event or on public transportation are taken, offer your seat to a woman or an elderly man. If the woman says "no thank you", stand up anyway and insist that she takes your seat.

Ladies

Table 9-2

	When a man opens the car door for you to enter, after you sit down, reach over to push his car door open.
	Ensure your conversations at dinner are appropriate for the occasion and never use profanity, talk politics or religion.
	Safe conversations to discuss with strangers are family, school, college choices, or careers after college.
	Allow the man to open the door for you, don't chastise him for being a gentleman, he knows that you can open your own door.
	Resist the urge to get angry or bring correction to your significant other in public, save the argument for when you get home.

Many young people may find themselves at a formal dinner because of sports and other community activities. See the table etiquette information below:

TOP NOTCH TABLE ETIQUETTE

1. Place your napkin in your lap as soon as you sit down at the table.
2. Sit up straight.
3. No elbows on the table.
4. *DO NOT* begin eating until everyone has been served.
5. Chew with your mouth closed.
6. No cell phones on the table.
7. If you need to make a phone call, excuse yourself from the table and make your call outside of the banquet room.

BREAD PLATE

1. Bread plate is to your left.
2. Place a nice portion of butter onto your plate, so you don't have to keep dipping into the communal plate.
3. Break off one bite size piece of bread at a time and butter it just before eating.

WATER GLASS

1. Water glass is to the right of your plate.
   Tip: Your left hand forms a "b" (bread plate) and your right hand forms a "d" (drink).

UTENSILS

1. As your courses come, use the utensils farthest away from your plate.
2. If there is a second fork at the top of your plate, this is for desserts.
3. When finished eating, lay your utensils at 11:00 o'clock position, tops pointing up
4. If one of your utensils falls on the floor, quietly get the servers attention to remove it.
5. NEVER, EVER, put a dirty utensil on the table.

SALT AND PEPPER OR BREAD

1. If someone asks for salt/pepper or bread, hand it over immediately, even if you haven't used it yet.
2. Place the salt/pepper on the table beside the person who will pass it to the person who requests it. Always place the salt/pepper on the table, do not put it their hand.
3. Pass both salt and pepper at the same time.
4. Do not season your food without tasting it first.
5. Don't OVER SEASON it, it looks childish.
6. Eating Soup
7. Eat soup by skimming the surface of the broth away from you, then bring it to your lips, lightly sipping without slurping.
8. HOT SOUP!! Do not blow it, wait until it cools.
9. When finished, rest the spoon on your plate. If the soup bowl came with a saucer, rest the spoon on it.

SALAD

Cut the leaves of the salad, one bite at a time. Don't hack up your salad all at once.

REMOVING FOOD FROM YOUR MOUTH

Remove food the same way it entered your mouth, by gently spitting it back on your fork and placing it on the edge of your plate. Resist the urge to spit it in your napkin.

FINISHED EATING

1. Lay your utensils at 11:00 o'clock position, tips pointing up.
2. If you need to pause or step away from the table momentarily, cross your utensils with the knife on your right AND put your napkin in your chair.
3. When finished, the napkin goes on the left of your dinner plate.

QUESTIONS:

1. If your fork falls on the floor during dinner, should you pick it up and put it on the table?

   YES | NO

2. When should you sit at the head of the table?

   _____

   _____

SPIRITUAL REFERENCE:

"What is desired in a man is kindness, And a poor man is better than a liar."
- **Proverbs 19:22 (NKJV)**

FAMOUS QUOTE:

"I think the thing I miss most in our age is our manners. It sounds so old-fashioned in a way. But even bad people had good manners in the old days, and manners hold a community together, and manners hold a family together; in a way, they hold the world together."
- **Nancy Friday**

TAKEAWAYS:

1. Displaying manners and kindness and being respectful will open doors for you.

2. Always show respect for your teachers, coaches, and leaders in public, even if you have a personal relationship with them.

AFFIRMATIONS: (Recite each morning)

I am a kind and respectful person.

TIME TO SOAR:

Exercise 1: BE KIND

Materials needed: Phone

1. If you are in a classroom environment, break up into groups of four, if not, go to your local grocery or department store.

2. In the classroom:
   - Practice giving two compliments to everyone in the group. Take turns until everyone has completed the exercise.

3. At the local grocery or department store:
   - Walk around the store and give four people a genuine compliment. You can compliment their shoes, hair, jewelry, suit, dress, jeans, how cute or well-mannered their children are etc.

This exercise will make people feel good about themselves and make them smile. Many times, kind comments can last in a person's heart for many years.

"Have courage and be kind."

- Cinderella Movie, 2015

Chapter 10

PREPARE FOR EMPLOYMENT

"Choose a job you love, and you will never have to work a day in your life."

- Confucius

When preparing for employment, you will most likely have to go through a job interview. The first question that will be asked of you is, "tell me about yourself?" This is an opportunity to highlight your achievements. This is not the time to talk about your hobbies, how many siblings you have, or how good you are at playing video games like "Fortnite". It is important for you to create a 30-second elevator pitch.

The information below will help you develop your elevator pitch:

Your Name: _____

(Roderick Cunningham)

Your High School: _____

(William Raines High School)

Your Clubs/Organizations: _____

(JROTC Squad Leader, Basketball Team Captain and Student Council Treasurer)

Favorite Subjects: _____

(Math)

Volunteer Activities: _____

(Tutoring elementary school students and reading to Senior citizens)

College you plan to attend: _____

(Florida State University)

College Major: _____

(Engineering)

Professional Strengths: _____

(Leader, team player and organized)

What can you offer? _____

(Excellent customer service and attention to detail)

Here's how to put it all together in a 30-second elevator pitch:

Interviewer: Hello, my name is Jim. Thank you for coming in to interview for our open position as a cashier. Before we get started, I would like to know more about you. Can you tell me a little about yourself?

You: Good morning Sir, my name is Roderick Cunningham. I am a senior at Raines High School where I am a squad leader with the Junior Reserve Officers Training Corps. Additionally, I am Team Captain of our varsity basketball team, and last year I was student council treasurer.

My favorite subject is math and I love volunteering at Long Elementary where I tutor 3rd graders in math. Last year I spent 40 volunteer hours reading to senior citizens at a local senior living facility. I plan to attend Florida State University in the fall, majoring in chemical engineering. I am an excellent leader, team player, and I am very organized. I think I could be a major asset to your organization because of my exceptional customer service skills and my ability to stay focused and pay attention to detail.

Interviewer: Wow! Impressive. Let me tell you about the position.

Very few young people are prepared with a 30-second elevator pitch when interviewing. This short pitch is so impressive that many interviewers will began to talk for the rest of the interview and may offer you the job on the spot. If you were the first interviewed, everyone else will not compare to you, if you are last, you will blow away the competition.

Professional Strengths:

Table 10-1 (Check all that apply)

	Team player		Strong computers and technology skills
	Smart		Decision maker
	Intelligent		Organizational skills
	Leader		Trustworthy
	Analytical		Collaborative
	Shows initiative		Diligent
	Speaks multiple languages		Communications skills
	Adaptable		Persistent
	Punctual		Resourceful
	Problem-Solver		Strong work ethic
	Flexible		Personable
	Organized		Planner
	Creative		Thinker
	Self-starter		Dependable
	Quick learner		Respect for authority

To make your strengths even more powerful, use the following words in front of the words above: *Excellent, highly, very, extremely, strong, incredible, effective, and keen.*

What can you offer a company?

Table 10-2 (Check all that apply)

	Customer service skills		Attention to detail
	Calmness under pressure		Completion of projects on-time
	Ability to build strong teams		Ability to recognize a problem and take action to solve it
	Ability to work well in a team environment		Self-less leadership
	Ability to organize events		Ability to organize people
	Ability to lead projects		Ability to negotiate contracts
	Work well with vendors and contractors		Understands multiple languages

Volunteer activities (Shows kindness, sympathy, and your willingness to serve others)

Table 10-3 (Check all that apply)

	Reading to elementary school kids		Feeding the homeless
	Tutoring elementary school kids		Working w/babies at local hospitals
	Volunteering at your church		School/community clean-up
	Reading to the Senior citizen community and planning fun activities		Create a youth sports camp (after school or during summer)
	Motivational speaking for younger kids (no drugs, work hard, listen to your parents, stay focused)		Volunteer to grocery shop for senior citizens in your community

Clubs/organizations or school sporting activities (Shows maturity, your ability to lead others, how well you work well in a team environment, and highlights positive social skills)

Table 10-4 (Check all that apply)

	JROTC - Junior Reserve Officer Training Corps (Leadership skills)		Sports: Volleyball, football, basketball, track and field, softball/baseball, etc.
	Clubs: Chess, art, drama, film, science, math, literature, language, charity, etc.		Chorus, band, orchestra, cheerleading, etc.
	Junior Firefighter		National Youth Leadership Council
	Boys/Girls Scouts of America		Big Brother Big Sisters of America
	DECA (Future leaders and entrepreneurs)		AVID - Advancement Via Individual Determination (College readiness)

Fraternity Groups w/programs for boys: - Omega Psi Phi - Alpha Phi Alpha - Kappa Alpha Psi - Phi Beta Sigma	Sorority Groups w/programs for girls: - Alpha Kappa Alpha - Delta Sigma Theta - Sigma Gamma Rho - Zeta Phi Beta
Junior Chamber of Commerce (Future business leaders)	Key Club (Leadership through serving others)
Civil Air Patrol Program or EAA Young Eagles Program (Future pilots/aviators)	The First Tee (Leadership through golf)
FBLA - Future Business Leaders of America	Urban League Leadership and Youth Programs (Summer and year-round)

Write-out your 30-second elevator pitch below:

_____

_____

_____

_____

_____

_____

_____

_____

_____

_____

_____

_____

_____

_____

_____

_____

_____

_____

_____

Resume Outline

Your Name: _____

Street Address: _____

City, State, Zip Code: _____

Phone: _____

(Cell Phone OK. Ensure a professional message is recorded)

Summary: _____

(Write a professional paragraph about you, very similar to your 30-second elevator pitch)

Skills and Strengths: _____

_____

(See Table 8-1 and 8-2)

Education/Honors/Clubs/Awards: _____

_____

_____

(High school name, GPA if above 3.0, Junior Honor Society, JROTC Squad Leader, basketball team captain and Student Council Treasurer)

Volunteer Activities: _____

(Tutoring elementary school students and reading to Senior Citizens)

Job Experience:

1. _____

2. _____

3. _____

4. _____

(Company name, position held, city, state, and dates of employment)

Duty Descriptions:

Company 1. _____

_____

_____

Company 2. _____

_____

_____

Company 3. _____

_____

_____

(Position held and duties performed)

Job Search

The most effective way to find new and/or better employment is through networking. I have seen people send out 300 resumes online, but only get an interview and eventually hired based on the recommendation of a family member or friend. Below is a list of people who can give you a great recommendation for employment:

1. Your parents
2. Your pastor
3. Your aunts/uncles
4. Your teachers/coaches
5. Your friends
6. Your previous coworkers
7. Your significant other's parents, family, friends, teachers, etc.

8. Social Media: Do a social media search for the company and see if any of your social media friends are employed there.

If you don't ask, you will never know if someone can help you. You will be surprised at the number of doors that will open once you start letting people know that you are looking for new employment.

Your friends will get you in the door by getting you the interview. You must always take the time necessary to prepare for an interview. Most people prepare for up to 8 hours for one interview. Here are some interview questions you should be prepared to answer:

Table 10-3

1. Can you tell me a little about yourself?	15. How did you hear about the position?
2. What do you know about the company?	16. Why do you want this job?
3. Why should we hire you?	17. What are your greatest professional strengths?
4. What do you consider to be your weaknesses?	18. What is your greatest professional achievement?
5. Tell me about a challenge or conflict you've faced at work, and how you dealt with it?	19. Where do you see yourself in five years?
6. What is your dream job?	20. What other companies are you interviewing with?
7. Why are you leaving your current job?	21. Why were you fired?
8. Why are you looking for a new position?	22. What type of work environment do you prefer?
9. What's your management style?	23. What's a time you exercised leadership?
10. Tell me about a time when you disagreed with a leader's decision at work?	24. How would your boss and co-workers describe you?
11. Why was there a gap in your employment?	25. Can you explain why you changed career paths?
12. How do you deal with pressure or stressful situations?	26. What would your first 30, 60, or 90-days look like in this role?
13. What is your salary requirements?	27. What do you like to do outside of work?

14. If you were an animal, which one would you want to be?	28. Do you have any questions for us?

Source: www.themuse.com

The questions above can be easily answered with the use of the internet, so I won't waste time here giving you the answer.

Professional organizations that can help in our success:

Table 10-4

	1. Develop a professional presence on LinkedIn®	*Network with other professionals through* **LinkedIn®**. *It helps with finding employment and other professional interests. You can also request an introduction from your* **LinkedIn®** *friend to a potential employer.*
	2. Volunteer with a Private Organization (hold an executive position)	*Fraternal, masonic, civic, JAYCEES, Kiwanis Club, Rotary Club, etc.*
	3. Volunteer to make a difference in the community	*Work with youth, sports, homeless, elderly, etc. Volunteering is the quickest way to find your purpose.*

In today's society, we must always tell the truth on our resume and on our social media sites. It is too easy to verify information on a person's resume. Don't ever lie about your education, job title, or companies worked for. Once you are caught lying, your reputation can be destroyed for a long time. It is not worth the hassle.

Quitting Your Job

Never allow your emotions to cause you to get fired or to quit your job. When you decide to leave your employment, it should be a well thought out moment that takes days or weeks to execute. First, you want to ensure that you have a new job, before you leave your old job. "NEVER quit a job before you get a new job." It is easier to find new employment when you already have a job, than to find new employment without a job. Don't cause yourself or your family a financial hardship because you are frustrated or because you don't like your supervisor.

Some people who may be in a deep emotional hole may find it difficult to take direction from supervisors. Your supervisor may ask you to do three big projects within the same hour and you may get very overwhelmed at this request. If this is you, climbing out of the emotional hole may be your first priority. Refer to my first book, *CLIMB: Face Your Past, Own Your Future*. If you are easily agitated by your leaders, if you speak negatively about them and disrespect them on a regular basis, and if you have secret thoughts of punching them in the face, then you will definitely want to refer to the book.

QUESTIONS:

1. Do you have a reputation of being honest, respectful, and hardworking?
   YES | NO, DON'T CARE | WORKING ON IT

2. Does your social media presence depict you as honest, respectful, hardworking?
   YES | NO, DON'T CARE | WORKING ON IT

3. If I used Google® to search your name, what would I find about you?

   _____

4. If I reached out to your high school teachers/counselors or your college professors and told them that I wanted to hire you for a job paying $500,000 per year, would they tell me good things about you?
   YES | NO | I DON'T KNOW | I HOPE SO

SPIRITUAL REFERENCE:

"For even when we were with you, we commanded you this: If anyone will not work, neither shall he eat. For we hear that there are some who walk among you in a disorderly manner, not working at all, but are busybodies."
- **II Thessalonians 3:10-11**

FAMOUS QUOTE:

"Whenever you are asked if you can do a job, tell 'em, 'Certainly I can!' Then get busy and find out how to do it."
–Theodore Roosevelt

TAKEAWAYS:

1. Manage your emotions! Do not quit your job before you get a new job.

2. Spend at least eight hours preparing for an interview. Practice answering interview questions with a family member.

AFFIRMATIONS: *(Recite each morning)*

1. I am kind and smart.
2. I will get a job offer after every interview.

TIME TO SOAR:

Exercise 1: DEVELOP YOUR RESUME

Materials needed: Computer with Microsoft Word®

Use the information you provided in this chapter's exercises to develop your resume. See the sample below:

1234 East Richmond Avenue | Jacksonville, FL 32219
PHONE 904-123-4567 | RogerSmith.Student@gmail.com

ROGER SMITH

SUMMARY

- High school senior with a 3.5 GPA
- Customer-focused self-starter with proven client service skills
- Responsible and dependable with high levels of professionalism
- Quick learner with attention to detail
- Excellent team player who thrives in teamwork situations
- Holds several leadership positions in school organizations and volunteers in the community

EDUCATION

- High School Diploma, Raines High School, Jacksonville, FL, expected May 2024

HONORS AND DISTINCTION

- Principal's Honor Roll, 2022 and 2023
- JROTC Leadership Award, 2023
- City Champs, Varsity Basketball, 2023

WORK HISTORY

Bagger, Kroger Markets, Jacksonville, FL, Summer 2023

- Greeted and provided customer service to 500 customers weekly
- Prepared bagged groceries to customer specifications
- Assisted in loading groceries to customer vehicles
- Assisted in unloading new merchandise and stocked shelves

Campaign Assistant, School Board Candidate, Jacksonville, FL, Fall, 2023

- Delivered campaign literature to 1200 families
- Spoke with 300 residents about the candidate's platform
- Answered phones at campaign headquarters
- Walked 30+ miles to get the message to the community

COMMUNITY SERVICE

- Supplied 60+ community service hours at Lakeview Senior Living Facility, Jan-Jun 2023
- Provided 50+ hours of tutoring to 8-year-olds at Branch Elementary School, Jul-Sep 2023

Chapter 11

YOU ARE BRILLIANT

"There's always going to be someone out there... who doesn't believe in you or who thinks your head is too big or you're not smart enough. But those are the people you need to ignore, and those are the times you need to just keep doing what you love doing.

- Jimmy Fallon

Just in case you haven't heard it lately, "you are brilliant". You already have what it takes to have massive success in your life, however, you may be lacking exposure to all the possibilities that exist. If you read, understand, and apply the principles from this book, plus graduate from high school, you will be well on your way!

As we grow up in our families and in school, we are taught that successful people are perfect, highly educated, and very intelligent. This is not true. Successful people are *not* perfect, in fact, many have negative traits, but "*lazy*" is not one of them. Successful people grind daily, they are committed, they work 12-18 hours per day and they take action...they make things happen! Many successful people are college educated, but others have informal education that they garnered from reading books, by surrounding themselves with intelligent people and learning from them, as well as being mentored by successful people. Mentors can show you the best way to accomplish your goals, and by doing so their education now becomes your education. Informal education is still education, but formal education (through colleges/universities) does the following:

1. Increases your confidence
2. Provides you with usable concepts and knowledge
3. Helps with your maturity
4. Helps you develop and expand your mind
5. Helps you develop a large network of lifelong friendships
6. Helps you realize what your capabilities are
7. Helps you understand the pitfalls of your personal and professional life
8. Allows you to tap into your unlimited potential and obtain knowledge

9. Gives you specialized knowledge

10. Helps you navigate life more efficiently

11. Shows that you can finish what you start

12. Helps you learn time management

13. Helps you learn how to manage projects effectively

14. Helps you develop team building skills

15. Helps you tap into your leadership potential

Although I am a proponent of formal education, I know that you can have everything above without a Bachelor's or Master's degree, but you will have to get the knowledge and skills from somewhere. Additionally, you will have to work twice as hard to prove to a potential employer or business investor that you are capable. The list below highlights a few ways you can overcome not having a formal education:

1. Find a mentor and learn from them.

2. Become an expert by reading two books per week for two-years on the same subject.

   - Healthcare Management
   - Psychology
   - Computer hacking/security
   - Stock market investing
   - Religion
   - Fashion design
   - Marketing

   - Life/business coaching
   - Sales
   - Criminal justice
   - Pilot
   - Entrepreneurship
   - Social work
   - Community activism

3. Create a vision board (see Section II).

4. Read your daily affirmations twice per day (see Section II).

5. Review your short and long-term goals twice daily (see Section II).

6. Develop your purpose statement (read "CLIMB: Face Your Past, Own Your Future").

7. Read "*Think and Grow Rich*" and follow the success system that is laid out.

8. Read "*7 Habits of Highly Effective People*".

9. Listen to motivational speakers at least 4 times per week.

10. Turn off the television and music that does not edify others.

11. Meditate daily and always keep dreaming of a better future (see Section II).

The idea behind this section is for you to feel just as confident and capable as a person with a degree. It will not be easy to overcome not having one but remember that you are not defined by the degrees on your wall, but by how you treat people, how you love and care for your family, and by the legacy you leave.

In my first book, **CLIMB: Face Your Past, Own Your Future**, my quest was to help you understand how your past hurts and lack of unconditional love is guiding some of your poor decision making. The first book was not written for you to blame others, but for you to recognize the past and make new and better decisions for your future. If I know that every time I drink a soda that I will have unbearable stomach pains for 2 days, then I will stop drinking sodas. Similarly, if I know that my anger stems from my relationship or lack of a relationship with my mother or father, then I will take action to be more understanding of their past emotional pain (stemming from parental abandonment, loss, trauma, and/or rejection). I would reach out to them and allow a better relationship to develop or simply control my feelings toward the relationship, but I would not let it continue to make me angry or sad. Be sure that you, and not your parents, children, friends, spouse, or employer are in control of your own emotions.

IQ versus EQ[10]

Many of you have heard of Intelligence Quotient (IQ) but you may not have heard of Emotional Quotient (EQ).

IQ is a score derived from taking a standardize test designed to assess intelligence. Intelligence is your capacity for abstract thought, logic, understanding, communication, learning, emotional knowledge, memory, creativity, planning, problem solving, and self-awareness.

The IQ ranges are below, according to www.assessmentpsychology.com:

Table 11-1

IQ Range	Classification	Theoretical Normal Curve
146+	Genius or near genius	0.1%
130-145	Very superior	2.1%
120-129	Superior	6.7%
110-119	High Average	16.1%
90-109	Average	50%
80-89	Low Average	16.1%
70-79	Borderline	6.7%
60-69	Extremely low	2.1%
Below 59	Mentally deficient	0.1%

According to the site, 97% of all people, of all races, scored between 70-145. Only 2.2% are below a 70. If you are mentally deficient, you would already know by now. Since you are capable of reading this book, you are not mentally deficient, you know how to follow directions, so you are capable of being highly successful and living the life YOU want. No more excuses.

EQ is the ability to identify, assess and control your own emotions or the emotions of others and of groups. Some people consider IQ as book smarts and EQ as street smarts.

According to www.psychcentral.com, there are five categories of emotional intelligence (EQ):

1. **Self-awareness:** The ability to recognize an emotion as it happens.

2. **Self-regulation:** You often have little control over when you experience emotions. You can however have some say in how long an emotion will last by using techniques to alleviate negative emotions such as anger, anxiety, or sadness.

3. **Motivation:** Creating clear goals and having a positive attitude.

4. **Empathy:** The ability to recognize how people feel is important to success in your life and career.

5. **Social Skills:** Development of good interpersonal skills, team building, collaboration skills, building bonds, and having influence over others.

Over the last 24 months, I 've mentored/coached 128 African-American and Latino boys from five elementary/middle schools in St. Petersburg, FL. As I attend all types of events that concern inner-city children in the community, I've heard people refer to minority kids as if they are not as intelligent as their white counterparts. What I have found is that these children have the same IQ as other children, but some of the inner-city children are unbalanced emotionally and socially based on parental abandonment, loss, trauma, and/or rejection. Many school districts are now recognizing this and are implementing Social Emotional Learning in the school system.

> *Social Emotional Learning (SEL) is the process through which children and adults acquire and effectively apply the knowledge, attitudes, and skills necessary to understand and manage emotions, set and achieve positive goals, feel and show empathy for others, establish and maintain positive relationships, and make responsible decisions. (www.caSEL.org)* [09]

If you look closely at the definition above as defined by the Collaborative for Academic Social, and Emotion Learning (caSEL), it is closely aligned with the five EQ categories above:

1. Effectively apply the knowledge, attitudes, and skills necessary to understand and manage emotions = **Self-awareness**

2. Set and achieve positive goals = **Motivation**

3. Feel and show empathy for others = **Empathy**

4. Establish and maintain positive relationships = **Social skills**

5. Make responsible decisions = **Self-regulation**

Inner-city children's EQ stifles the IQ, making the children too emotional to recognize and display their overall intelligence. In other words, their up and down emotional state is smothering their IQ and it may take them a long time to realize how smart they truly are. Some never realize it, some will figure it out in a prison cell, while others figure it out in their 30s and go on to enormous success in their lives.

So, what do we do? We have to focus on balancing the emotions of parents at home, which could affect the emotional balance of multiple children in the home, which will lead to children paying attention to the teachers, leading to higher test scores on standardized tests, leading to less frustrated children, leading to a more balanced teenager, leading to a more balanced and successful adult, leading to economic excellence in our communities.

I have found that some of our African-American youth in the inner-city may not know where their next meal is coming from. Some parents don't help or are not capable of helping with homework because they dropped out of school themselves (due to parental abandonment, loss, trauma, or rejection). Some 5th grade children may be required to pick-up their younger siblings from school, cook dinner, help their siblings with homework, wash dishes, clean the whole house, and wash clothes because their mother or grandmother works two or more part-time jobs, is sick with a debilitating disease, is very lazy, or may be using drugs.

Speaking from personal experience, no one, besides my mother, ever told me that I was smart. I didn't hear that until I joined the Air Force and was working at my first duty station at Ramstein Air Base, Germany. Hearing my supervisor, Staff Sergeant Charles Chinnis, say, *"Wow, Airman Cunningham, you are a smart guy and you do great work,"* was music to my ears. His words encouraged me to succeed and to win many honors, awards, and decorations throughout my 29-year military career. The confidence I gained from having other men speak positively into my life helped me to focus and attain three degrees and to start working on a fourth.

The point here is simple. Young people need heavy encouragement from their parents, teachers, and leaders. Parents' overall emotional health is key to their children's emotional health. Once the household finds emotional balance, everyone's intelligence can rise up and thrive.

SPIRITUAL REFERENCE:

"For I know the plans I have for you," declares the Lord, "plans to prosper you and not to harm you, plans to give you hope and a future."
- **Jeremiah 29:11 (NIV)**

FAMOUS QUOTE:

1. "The successful entrepreneurs that I see have two characteristics: self-awareness and persistence. They're able to see problems in their companies through their self-awareness and be persistent enough to solve them.
   - Alan Schaaf

2. "We have self-centered minds which get us into plenty of trouble. If we do not come to understand the error in the way we think, our self-awareness, which is our greatest blessing, is also our downfall.
   - Joko Beck

TAKEAWAYS:

1. You are smart enough to have enormous success in high school, college, career, and life. Get a mentor, get committed, educate yourself, READ, and take massive action.

2. Emotional Intelligence is identified through self-awareness, self-regulation, empathy, social skills, and motivation. Social Emotional Learning was created around emotional intelligence and is being rolled out in school districts all over the nation to help students with emotional isolation.

AFFIRMATIONS: (Recite each morning)

I am highly intelligent

TIME TO SOAR:

Exercise 1: TAKE A PERSONALITY TEST

Materials needed: Smartphone or Internet Access

To understand your personality better, take the Jung/Myers-Briggs Personality Test. The test will teach you more about why you do what you do. It is a 64-question test that takes 6-12 minutes to take. It is time well spent.

1. Go to www.humanmetrics.com |
2. Select "Personality Test - Jung/Myers-Briggs Types"
3. Then select "Take the Test!"

Instructions: When responding to the statements, please choose the response you agree with most. If you are not sure how to answer, make your choice based on your most typical response or feeling in the given situation. Selecting an upper case "YES" means strong agreement and checking a lower case "yes" means moderate agreement. Likewise, selecting an upper case "NO" means strong disagreement, and checking a lower case "no" means moderate disagreement. Selecting "uncertain" means you do not feel strongly either way about the given situation. To get a reliable result, please respond to all questions.

4. When you are done, press the "Score It!" button at the bottom of the screen.

5. What is your Myers-Briggs **_TYPE_** Indicator? _____

6. Percentages: _____ | _____ | _____ | _____

7. Select your **_TYPE_** DESCRIPTION and read it.

8. Go back to your score browser tab and select CAREERS. What career types were listed for you?

_____

_____

9. Feel free to Google your **_TYPE_** and read other descriptions of your personality.

SECTION II

CREATE A ROUTINE OF HEALTHY LIVING

"Psychology, unlike chemistry, unlike algebra, unlike literature, is an owner's manual for your own mind. It's a guide to life. What could be more important than grounding young people in the scientific information that they need to live happy, healthy, productive lives? To have good relationships?"

- Daniel Goldstein

Chapter 12

START WITH A HEALTHY MIND

"People are basically the same the world over. Everybody wants the same things - to be happy, to be healthy, to be at least reasonably prosperous, and to be secure. They want friends, peace of mind, good family relationships, and hope that tomorrow is going to be even better than today.

- Zig Ziglar

In order to create massive change in your life, you must be REBIRTHED. Your rebirthing process starts with a renewed MIND, BODY, and SPIRIT. If you have completed the exercises laid out in **CLIMB:** *Face Your Past, Own Your Future*, then this chapter will show you how to stay focused, maintain your enthusiasm, reach your goals, and create an amazing life for yourself and your family.

In the United States, we live in a stressful, fast-paced nation. When stressed, we tend to reach for something in our lives that gives us comfort. The things we reach for aren't necessarily healthy. Under stress, we can reach for alcohol, cigarettes, drugs, sex, fighting, gossiping about others, unhealthy romantic relationships, profane music, unhealthy foods, too many hours of video gaming, too many hours of reading, spending too much money shopping, etc.

Although we live in a nation that is very hectic and fast-paced, we must take time to maintain good health. Stress can set the stage for poor eating and less exercise. If you have a poor diet, you may run the risk of gaining weight or possibly find yourself with a chronic disease like high blood pressure, high cholesterol, or diabetes. Not sleeping well, smoking, and/or drinking can also lead to the risk of negative effects on your health which normally starts to manifest in your body by the age of 35. Your choice to maintain a healthy body will lead you in making healthy choices in multiple areas of your life.

Renew Your MIND Daily

To renew your mind, you must continue to set goals, visualize your future, read self-help books, take actions recommended by your mentor/coach, think and speak in a positive manner, and eliminate stress. The hardest part here is eliminating stress. You must put on the "*full armor of God*" before you leave your home each day. You can do this by learning how to control your mind. Only you and God should have control over your mind and thoughts, not your father who won't call you back, or your mother who talks down to you, or your grandmother who passed away, or the Uncle who touched you inappropriately. If you can get your mind right, you can get everything right.

To eliminate stress is to understand a few things about people and life:

1. Everything happens for a reason. We may not understand the reason just yet, but it will reveal itself in an hour, week, month, or years later. Trust the process and don't question every perceived bad thing that happens to you. Everything that happened is now history. Don't get angry or sad, just figure out what ~~do~~ you need to do to FIX IT or LEARN from it. How many bad things have you survived over your life? You made it through those times and you will make it through this time. Don't waste time pouting, fighting, being sad, having anxiety, etc. Everyone else has moved on and you're still mad.

2. Most people really want to be helpful, but they don't know how to do it, so they may offend you. We can't expect everyone to think with their hearts, some will think with their heads and mess everything up, although they didn't mean to.

3. Most people don't know that they have offended you. If you express to them that they have offended you, then you have done your part. If you do not let them know that you were offended, then how can the situation ever be corrected? Learn lessons of strength, power, and understanding from the situation and move on. You know you have moved on when negative emotions are no longer conjured up from the thought of the person, event or situation.

4. Never allow someone to control whether your family has food, clothing, or shelter. It is very stressful to be fired or laid off. You should consider yourself a contractor for the company you are working for. When the contract is over, you have others waiting to contract your services. In other words, you have to see yourself as a company with many options, instead of an employee with one option. Seven (7) streams of income can help ensure that one organization or one person is not in charge of your family's future. Always have a backup plan.

5. Love hard but understand that a romantic partner can wake up one day and decide that they would like to go their separate way. Many people have 5 or more serious relationships before they get married, but if you want to keep your relationship, fight for it! Work hard to keep it if you want it. Do your part to ensure that the relationship is healthy. Seek counseling if you want to keep the relationship going. Cheating on your significant other is an issue of mental isolation. Some people find comfort in drugs, alcohol, and gambling, while others find comfort in flirting or having sexual relations outside of their committed relationship. The strategies to deal with this fact is explained in my first book, *"CLIMB: Face Your Past, Own Your Future."* In other words, eliminate stress, eliminate cheating. If you are married, you made the vow, "for richer or poorer, in sickness and in health". Cheating is a mental health issue, mental health is a sickness, so cheating is a sickness. It's time to get medical help, it is not time to get a divorce and destroy the family structure.

So how do we achieve all of our dreams? It is actually quite simple. You must create new habits to control your thinking. Every morning when you wake up, you must do the following if you want dramatic change in your life:

20 mins: **Feed your spirit**: Pray, meditate, and read your spiritual guide (Bible for me)

- Spirituality is a very broad concept and includes a sense of connection to something bigger than ourselves.
- Everyone is spiritual, some more than others.
- Many will connect their spirituality to religion.
- Religion is a set of rules/rituals that provide you with a connection for your spirit, which is looking to attach itself.

1 min: Review your **Vision Board**

2 mins: Review your **Goals**

2 mins: Recite your **Daily Affirmations**

3 mins: Meditate on your future through the **Visualization Exercise**

2 mins: Recite your **Gratefulness List**

This takes only 30 minutes per day. If waking up 30 minutes early and putting on the full armor of God **guaranteed** that you would achieve your dreams, would you get up early?

Do you constantly tell your brain that you are not a morning person and that this could never happen for you?

You must push yourself every day to keep your mind sharp. Don't allow negative thoughts to control your day, this will take work, but you are worth it.

Create a Vision Board

Vision boards are very helpful in moving you in the direction of your goals and dreams. Your vision board is a series of pictures representing where you see your life going over the next 20 years. Your vision board will change as you learn and grow in your spirituality, your family, your life, and your career. Your vision board can be on a poster board or it can be created on the computer and printed out poster-size at your nearest office supply store or business printing company. It could include pictures of the following:

1. Dream home
2. Dream kitchen
3. Dream pool
4. Dream quiet space for reading, meditation and prayer
5. Dream spouse (be careful not to replace your current spouse)
6. Dream kids (have fun with that one)
7. Dream college (i.e. banners or caps with your favorite college's logo)
8. Dream car
9. Dream vacation
10. Dream business, career, or position
11. Dream lifestyle
12. Dream daily activities (i.e. bike riding, exercising, walking on the beach, skiing, etc.)
13. Dream place of worship and providing service to others

The pictures should represent you between now and 20 years from now. Be sure to place your poster on your wall or on the back of the bathroom door. It should be anywhere that you will view it at least twice per day upon awaking and prior to going to bed.

"SAMPLE" VISION BOARD

DESIRE
+
BELIEF
+
ACTION
=
RESULTS!

Dream Home

Dream Kitchen

Dream Swimming Pool

$200K per year
in income by age 30

Bachelors Degree by age 22
Masters Degree by age 24
MD, J.D., or PhD by age 30

Quiet Space for Reading,
Praying and Meditating

Dream Family

Corporate CEO

Dream Wedding

Dream Vacation

Love and Relationship

MIAMI STATE
UNIVERSITY

Medical Nurse/Doctor

Entrepreneur

Dream Car

I BELIEVE I CAN DO THIS!

I pray that I learn HOW to control my
thoughts, it *WILL* dictate my future.
I will not allow negative people to
control my thoughts.

Develop Short-Term and Long-Term Goals

Goals are dreams with a deadline. When developing your goals, you should begin with thoughts of the end. What is your endpoint? Where do you see yourself personally, financially, professionally, educationally, and spiritually at the age of 40?

To help you focus on a particular area of interest, simply answer this question,

> *"If you were guaranteed success in any career field, what career field would you choose if I paid you $400,000 per year to do it."*

Some people are able to answer this question immediately, while others may take days, weeks, months, or even years to figure it out. Take a moment and ask your family and friends that exact same question, you will be amazed at how that question can stump a 40-year-old with a Master's Degree. Some will also state that they are not concerned about money but will depend on others who are concerned about money (i.e. parents, grandparents, siblings, aunt/uncle, etc.) to pay a bill or loan them money.

Short-term goals are goals you plan to achieve over the next 6 months to 1 year.

Examples of short-term goals:

Table 12-1

	PERSONAL /FITNESS/FINANCIAL
	I will increase my water intake from 2 glasses per day to four by Feb 1, 2022
	I will pay myself 30% of my paycheck before I pay anyone else (invest 10%, save 10%, and give 10% to church/charity) by Jun 1, 2022
	I will run 2-miles under 18 minutes by Jun 15, 2022
	I will start to treat my little brother with respect and mentor him to be successful, starting now.
	PROFESSIONAL
	I will land a $15 per hour part-time job by putting in 20 applications weekly by Aug 15, 2022
	I will read two books on leadership every month for the next 8 months, reading 16 books by March 1, 2022
	EDUCATIONAL
	I will graduate High School and attend college at Florida State University by Jun 1, 2022

I will retake my SATs to ensure a score of 1350 by Jan 1, 2022	
SPIRITUAL	
I will spend 30 minutes every night reading the Bible starting Monday	
I will volunteer to teach at the church's youth camp by Jun 18, 2022	

Long-term goals are goals you plan to achieve over the next 1 to 20 years. With long-term goals, you should block out 30 minutes each morning, close your eyes, and visualize your future at the age of 40. After that visualization exercise, you can work on the steps today to get you to your goal at the age of 40. For example, if you want to be a high school principal, then you must first have a Master's Degree and you must have spent years as a teacher. In order to be a teacher, you must have a Bachelor's degree. In order to have a Bachelor's Degree, you must go to college. In order to go to college, you must get excellent grades. In order to get excellent grades, you must minimize absences, study, and respect the education system. The things that you do today, will prepare you to become a high school principal at 40-years-old.

Examples of long-term goals:

Table 12-2

PERSONAL /FITNESS/FINANCIAL
I will be financially free with $5 million in investment assets by age 40
I will run in the Boston Marathon by age 30
PROFESSIONAL
I will run my own medical consulting business with revenues of $25 Million by age 35
I will become a pediatric nurse by age 24
EDUCATIONAL
I will have my Bachelors in Nursing by age 22
I will complete my Master's Degree in Nursing by age 25
SPIRITUAL
I will teach Bible Study by age 22
I will have read the entire Bible by age 20

Our minds have to be trained properly, so we have to write down our goals and read them daily. Additionally, whenever you sit down with your mentor, you should have your goals ready to display. Goals are the basic steps to realizing your success, so you must have these in place for anyone to take you seriously when it comes to achieving your goals.

1. Do you think that you should memorize your goals? Why or why not?

   _____

2. Should all goals have a date of completion? Why or why not?

   _____

YOUR GOALS

SHORT-TERM GOALS

	PERSONAL /FITNESS/FINANCIAL	Date or Age
	PROFESSIONAL	
	EDUCATIONAL	
	SPIRITUAL/COMMUNITY VOLUNTEERISM	

LONG-TERM GOALS

	PERSONAL /FITNESS/FINANCIAL	Date or Age
	PROFESSIONAL	
	EDUCATIONAL	
	SPIRITUAL/COMMUNITY VOLUNTEERISM	

DAILY AFFIRMATIONS

Below are samples of my daily affirmations that I read aloud each morning in the mirror for two minutes:

1. I PUT *GOD FIRST*, FAMILY SECOND, AND CAREER THIRD
2. I AM *KIND*, I *RESPECT* OTHERS, AND I *LOVE* EVERYONE
3. I AM STRONG, CONFIDENT, AND *I BELIEVE* IN MYSELF
4. I WILL *LEAD* MYSELF, MY CHILDREN, AND OTHERS
5. I AM *COMMITTED* TO ACHIEVING MY GOALS AND WILL HELP OTHERS ACHIEVE THEIRS
6. I *LOVE* MY SPOUSE AND *FAMILY* WITH ALL OF MY HEART AND SOUL
7. I WILL RESIST THE URGE TO JUDGE OTHERS AND WILL GO *WITHOUT JUDGEMENT* OF ANYTHING THAT OCCURS TODAY
8. I EXPECT A *HEALTHY MIND*, A HEALTHY *BODY*, AND A HEALTHY *SPIRIT*
9. I AM *HEALED* OF ALL SICKNESS IN MY BODY
10. I AM A *GIVER* AND I AM *HAPPY* WHEN OTHERS SUCCEED AND WIN
11. I CREATE *POSITIVE* RELATIONSHIPS THAT ARE *FAIR*, *HONEST*, AND *HEALTHY*
12. I EXPECT *WEALTH* AND *ABUNDANCE* EVERY DAY OF MY LIFE
13. I AM *SMART*, *INTELLIGENT*, AND I AM COLLEGE *FOCUSED*
14. I AM A PERSON WHO *LAUGHS* WITH CHILDISH JOY
15. I AM *RESPONSIBLE*, *TRUSTING*, *WISE* AND *KNOWLEDGEABLE*
16. I AM *DARING* AND *SUCCESSFUL*
17. I HAVE *UNLIMITED POWER* AT MY DISPOSAL
18. I AM *TEACHABLE* AND *TRAINABLE*
19. I AM IN *CONTROL* OF MY EMOTIONS AND I WILL NOT GIVE THAT CONTROL TO OTHERS
20. I AM *PREPARED* TODAY TO MEET MY FUTURE GOALS AND I HAVE A RESULTS-ORIENTED *ACTION PLAN*
21. *I LOVE* MYSELF, *I FORGIVE* MYSELF AND EVERYONE WHO HAS EVER HURT ME

YOUR DAILY AFFIRMATIONS

Start with I, I AM, or I WILL.

1.	
2.	
3.	
4.	
5.	
6.	
7.	
8.	
9.	
10.	
11.	
12.	
13.	
14.	
15.	
16.	
17.	
18.	
19.	
20.	

VISUALIZATION EXERCISE

Reflect over your future for 10 minutes each morning. Find a quiet space in your home and reflect and dream of an awesome future professionally, personally, financially, educationally, and spiritually.

THE TIMELINE OF YOUR LIFE

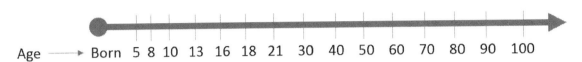

Age ➔ Born 5 8 10 13 16 18 21 30 40 50 60 70 80 90 100

If you are under 25, visualize your life at the age of 35. If you are over 30, visualize your life in 10 year intervals (i.e., if you are 50, visualize your life at 60).

Answer the following questions based on the age of 35 or in 10 years (whichever is later):

1. Home Type: 1-story | 2-story | Condo | Cottage | Mansion
2. City where you live: _____
3. Your profession: _____
   Position/Title: _____
4. Highest level of education: _____
5. # of cars: _____
   Type of Car #1_____ #2 _____
   #3 _____
6. Years of marriage: _____
7. Number of kids: _____ | # girls _____ # Boys _____
8. Age of your oldest child: _____

Note: This will help your mind focus on when you plan to start having children and if you plan to be married before you start to have children. If you are a teenager visualizing your life at 35 and you answer that your oldest child is 15, then you plan to start having children at the age of 20, getting pregnant at 19.

If you don't plan this in your mind, someone else will plan it for you.

Now it is time to visualize your future. After having someone read it to you the first couple of times, you will be able to do it alone.

YOUR VISUALIZATION EXERCISE

1. If you are in a classroom, break up into groups of two. If not in a classroom setting, ask someone to help you with this exercise.
2. Take turns reading the passage below to each other.
3. Use your most soothing voice for this exercise.
4. If time is a factor, the facilitator can read the passage below to ALL participants at the same time.
5. *Slowly* read the following passage in a soothing, yet serious tone to the participant:
    a. I want you to close your eyes

    b. It is very important that you keep your eyes closed throughout this exercise.

    c. Now, I want you to imagine your life at the age of 35-years-old.

    d. What is your profession? Are you a high school principal, a doctor, a lawyer, a business owner, a community leader, a retired athlete?

    e. What state or country do you reside in?

    f. What type of home do you live in? Is it a ranch style or two-story home or maybe a condo downtown or on the beach?

    g. Now, I want you to imagine yourself standing in front of your home. You should be able to see your home clearly in your mind's eye. I want you to walk up to your home and see your hand opening the front door. As you walk into your home, I want you to go to the left and enter the large kitchen area. The kitchen has a large island with elegant cabinets. The entire space is absolutely beautiful, just like you designed it. Your friends and family are in the kitchen and they are happy to see that you finally made it home. They give you hugs and kisses. As you proceed through the kitchen, you will make a right as you leave your dining room. You walk up to the sliding glass doors and open them. Your favorite cousin is in the pool with her kids and says, "Hello cousin, thanks for inviting us over, I love your place." You yell back, "It's great seeing you." As you close the sliding glass door, you turn around and your spouse is standing there with your children.

h. What does your spouse look like? Is he/she tall or short? What type of hair does he/she have? How does he/she smell? How does his/her voice sound? What accent or dialect do they use when speaking?

i. How many children do you have? How old are they? How many girls and how many boys do you have?

j. As you walk toward your spouse and children, you reach out to hug them and kiss them. Then you tell them that you will be back shortly.

k. As you walk upstairs and into your home office, you begin to admire your degrees on the wall. You admire your high school diploma where you graduated with honors. You admire your bachelor's and Master's, Degree from two of the top universities in America where you graduated summa cum laude (with the highest distinction) from both schools. You then walk over to take a close look at your Doctorate Degree hanging on the wall. You are extremely proud of this degree because of the hard work it took to achieve this goal.

l. You smile when you look at the "Key to the City" given to you by the Mayor for all your community service and advocacy work.

m. As you leave your office and go back downstairs, you decide to walk into your garage. There are three cars in your garage. I want you to slowly walk around the first car. What type of car is it? Is it a mini-van, a Honda, Mercedes, Bentley? As you move to the second car, take your time as you walk around it. What type of car is it? Now move on to the third car which is a sporty convertible; open the driver's door and get behind the wheel, let the top down, and lift up the garage door. Drive out of the garage and go to your office for a quick meeting with your staff.

n. When you arrive at the office, go in and let everyone know that they can have the rest of the day off and to enjoy their holiday weekend. Get back into your convertible and head home. Park in the driveway, get out of the car, and admire your home, think of your wonderful family, and the life you have built.

o. Now, open your eyes.

If you do this every single day, you WILL take control of your own thoughts and begin to put the action in place to live your dreams. This is how to condition your mind for success. It is POWERFUL!

GRATEFULNESS EXERCISE

Below is a sample list of things that I am grateful for today.

I am grateful that...

1. I love God and believe in his saving Grace and that his son Jesus died for our sins.
2. I love my wife, children, and grandchildren with all of my heart.
3. I have a beautiful wife and we have a loving and trusting relationship.
4. I am a confident person who believes in my abilities to care and provide for my family.
5. I am in good health and I am in good shape.
6. I am able to help others to succeed in life.
7. I am a good friend.
8. I have good taste in clothing.
9. All of my children are God-loving, independent, and they are in healthy relationships with someone who loves and respects them.
10. My wife and I have reliable transportation.
11. I have a beautiful, relaxing place to call home.
12. I have enough finances to sustain my lifestyle.
13. I don't judge others and are able to forgive everyone.
14. I have the gift to connect to other people.
15. I give freely of my time and monies.
16. I am able to help others in the name of my mother who taught me how to love people unconditionally.
17. I was raised in a loving, respectful household where my mother ALWAYS had my back.
18. I am able to love unconditionally.

YOUR GRATEFULNESS EXERCISE

List 20 things you are happy about in your life RIGHT NOW!

I am grateful that...

1.	
2.	
3.	
4.	
5.	
6.	
7.	
8.	
9.	
10.	
11.	
12.	
13.	
14.	
15.	
16.	
17.	
18.	
19.	
20.	

Diagram 12-1

RAISE D-BAR

Desire (Hope): A strong feeling of wanting to have something or wishing for something to happen.

Belief (Faith) : An acceptance that a statement is true or that something exists.

Action (Work): The fact or process of doing something, typically to achieve an aim.

Result (Manifestation): A consequence, effect, or outcome of something.

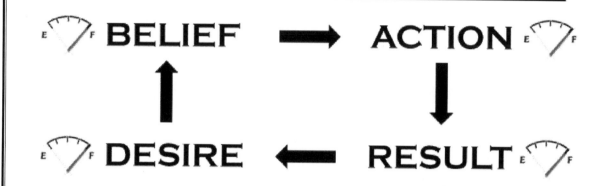

Anything that you want to accomplish (major or minor) in life can be done by using D-BAR.

Desire: Do you have a strong desire to accomplish this goal or attain something? Are you FULL of desire?

Belief: Do you truly believe that you can have what you want? Is it an insane belief? Are you FULL of belief or just HALF FULL of belief?

Action: What are you willing to do EXACTLY to accomplish your goal? It is great to have goals and dreams, but you must put activity behind it, otherwise you are hallucinating. Your action is what makes it real. When you are FULL of action, you will get acceptable results.

Result: Your results may not always be FULL, but if you decrease your action, you will never have full results. Eventually, when you are FULL of action, you will get FULL results and meet your goals and expectations.

You must always be full of Desire and Belief, which will lead to massive Action and exceptional Results. D-BAR never stops. We are always trying to attain something and we must go into Action to attain it.

Diagram 12-2

Make copies (use one sheet for each goal)

RAISE D-BAR

WEEKLY GOAL ACCOMPLISHMENT

Goal (Be Specific): _____

Examples:

Graduate from the University of Florida with a Bachelor's Degree in Business
Purchase a diamond ring for my girlfriend
Purchase my brand new Black E350 Mercedes-Benz
Upgrade my kitchen cabinets
Purchase a bicycle for my son
Increase sales in my company to $5 million annually
Lose 20 pounds by running 4 miles/3 times per week

Date You Plan to Accomplish the Goal: _____

What is that ACTION that you will take to attain this goal:_____

_____

_____

_____ **BELIEF** ➡️ **ACTION** _____
Level   Level
Empty - Full   Empty - Full

⬆️   ⬇️

_____ **DESIRE** ⬅️ **RESULT** _____
Level   Level
Empty - Full   Empty - Full

Level = Empty / ¼ / Half / ¾ / FULL

If your Desire is full and you have insane Belief, then you will take massive Action, giving you exceptional Results. If your Desire or Belief ever starts to fade, then your action and results will follow.

Trademark - Chief Empowerment Network, LLC 2016

Chapter 13

CREATE A HEALTHY BODY

"Follow your dreams, work hard, practice and persevere. Make sure you eat a variety of foods, get plenty of exercise and maintain a healthy lifestyle.

Sasha Cohen

Although today's world is very hectic and fast-paced, we must take time to maintain good health. Stress can set the stage for poor eating and less exercise. If you have a poor diet, you may run the risk of gaining weight or possibly find yourself with a chronic disease like high blood pressure, high cholesterol, or diabetes. Not sleeping well, smoking, and/or drinking can also lead to the risk of negative effects on your health, which normally starts to manifest in your body by the age of 35. Your choice to maintain a healthy body will lead you in making healthy choices in multiple areas of your life.

The three keys to creating a healthy body are:

- **Exercise**: Aerobic exercise and weightlifting.
- **Healthy Eating**: Cutting down on sodas, junk food, and fast food.
- **Lifestyle Changes**: Manage stress, stop smoking, meditate and get plenty of rest.

Exercise[11]

Table 13-1

Cardio	Walk, jog, and or run at least 3 times per week for 30 to 60 minutes. Small increases in distance and pace should occur weekly.
Strength Training	Lift weights at least 2 times per week. If you can't make it to the gym, do sit-ups and push-ups at home. It is not uncommon for men to start with 30 push-ups in 5 min, then within 90 days be at 200 push-ups in 5 min. Small increases in weight and reps should occur weekly.
Move Around	If you have an office job, it is important to get up from the computer and move around each hour for 2 minutes. Try not to disturb others.

Healthy Eating[11]

Table 13-2

Count Calories	A calorie is defined as a unit of energy supplied by food. A calorie is a calorie regardless of its source. Carbs, fats, sugars, or proteins, all contain calories.
Eat a Well-Balanced Diet	Eat food, different food daily, from the five different food groups. (1. Carbohydrates, 2. Protein, 3. Milk and dairy, 4. Fruit and vegetables, 5. Fats and sugars. Ensure you measure your portions.
Eat Lean Protein	Helps to maintain lean muscle mass, supports your immune system, and rebuilds cells. Includes poultry, eggs, seafood, tofu, legumes (nuts and beans). Try to avoid beef, and pork.
Make Half of Your Meal a fruit or vegetable	Fruits/Vegetables have been linked to decreased blood pressure, decreased risk of blindness, decreased risk of stroke and heart disease, and better management of blood sugar and heart disease.
Whole Grain Only	Brown rice (always eat rice in moderation due to arsenic found in most rice), 100% whole wheat pasta and bread, quinoa, barley, and whole grain oats.
No Junk Foods or Processed Foods	Consider taking left-overs to work/school and avoid fast-food restaurants. If you currently drink four sodas/sugary sports drinks daily, change it to two sodas/sports drinks daily.
Drink Plenty of Water	You should drink ten 8-oz glasses of water daily to avoid dehydration. Dehydration leads to fatigue, mental fogginess, urinary tract infections, kidney stones, and mood swings.

Take Vitamin and Mineral Supplements	If you eat a healthy diet, you do not need supplements. Supplements are there as a back-up for people who don't eat healthy foods or are temporarily unable to meet all of your nutrient needs through food.
Skip the Desert	If you eat dessert with lunch/dinner daily, change it to eating dessert once or twice per week.

Lifestyle Changes[11]

Table 13-3

	Stop Smoking	Smoking leads to blindness, diabetes, heart disease, high blood pressure, lung cancer, and mouth disease.
	Minimize Drinking	Heavy drinking (2-3 glasses per day) leads to high blood pressure, liver damage, brain damage, stroke, and pancreatitis.
	Get Enough Sleep	Sleep deprivation leads to weight gain, fatigue, poor concentration, increased hunger, and it can affect your ability to concentrate or retain information.
	Meditate Daily	Meditation can help to relieve stress and help you to focus on a more positive future for yourself and your family.
	Take Naps	For some, a short 30-45 minute nap can provide a burst of energy.
	Visit Your Doctor/ Dentist Regularly	We should all have a family doctor (primary care physician). Be sure to visit often so they can help you prevent any chronic illnesses. Also, dental checkups and cleanings should be done twice per year.

www.cdc.gov/healthyweight/[11]

"It is never too late to change the way you eat - once you do, your body will thank you with a longer and healthier life."

- David H. Murdock

Chapter 14

DEVELOP A HEALTHY SPIRIT

"You don't have to believe what I believe but believe in something outside of yourself."

\- Roderick Cunningham

If we are to have a healthy mind, body, and spirit, we have to speak about spirituality. Spirituality is a very broad concept and includes a sense of connection to something bigger than ourselves. If you ask 50 people to define spirituality, you will get 50 different answers. Spirituality and religion are two different, but complimentary concepts.

Spirituality:

- Where do I find meaning for my life?
- How do I feel connected to people, places, or things?
- How should I live my life?

Religion:

- What rituals should I follow?
- What is right and what is wrong?
- What is true and what is false?

Religions and religious organizations have developed systems, practices, and rituals to answer your questions on spirituality. Now, you have to decide which religion gives you comfort and aligns with your beliefs and ethics.

My personal belief is that we have three different spirits that dwell within us.

- The evil spirit that we call the devil or darkness
- The holy spirit that we call the angel or light
- The human spirit that makes you do things that feel good to you

Whichever spirit you feed the most, will be the spirit that comes out through your actions. For example:

1. If you listen to explicit (laced in profanity) rap or rock music, which spirit are you feeding?
2. If you look at pornographic images, which spirit are you feeding?
3. If you feed the homeless, which spirit are you feeding?
4. If you listen to gospel music that stirs your spirit, which spirit are you feeding?
5. If you read the Bible, which spirit are you feeding?

One of the three spirits will guide your life if you don't take control of your own life. If your spirit instructs you to *"punch him in the face,"* and you do just that, then you are most likely being guided by a dark spirit that we call the devil.

Your spirit is modified by what comes into your senses of touch, smell, taste, hearing, and seeing. We call these "gates" and you have to "GUARD YOUR GATES."

If you want to be guided by the light or the holy spirit, then you should study the book to learn the systems, practices, and rituals of your chosen religion, pray, meditate, and listen to spiritual music that connects with your soul. If you do this often, you will have less of the devil speaking softly in your head, and more of the holy spirit speaking softly in your head and guiding your life to success, happiness, and victory.

Have you ever met anyone that made your skin crawl? You may have said to yourself, *"oooh, I don't like his spirit at all"*.

Have you watched your new boyfriend/girlfriend enter a room and/or give you a certain kind of eye contact and you get butterflies in your stomach? That feeling means that your spirits are connected and that you are on the same vibration or frequency. Some operate on different frequencies, but when we meet someone on our same frequency, there is an instant connection and both people can feel it. That connection makes us say things like, *"our spirits just gelled immediately"*.

Have you ever heard someone sing and it gave you goosebumps? That means that you are on the same frequency and in total vibration with the singer. Everyone won't feel the same way. That's why we have so many genres of music. This 'vibe' or 'connection' applies to cars, homes, music, and people. Everyone likes what connects with them, certain models of cars, different style homes, different genres of music, different types of guys/girls, etc., based on their frequency.

If you don't connect your spirit to a religion, eventually you will connect it to something:

> Money, gangs, hate groups, devil worshippers, cults, profane music, negative people, etc.

What I find interesting is that when people claim to be atheist or agnostic (don't believe in the existence of God), I notice that when life gets extremely stressful, they call on Christians for advice or help. They will say things like, *"please pray for me"* or *"help me, tell me what to do, but please don't talk about Jesus"*. What I have found is that these people have experienced extreme parental abandonment, extreme loss, heavy trauma, or serious rejection and they can't seem to believe that God would allow this to happen to them or to their family.

What is the worst thing that could happen to someone who is a believer in God? Believers in God tend to treat people with kindness, love and respect. You forgive others and have faith that you will be forgiven. You gain wisdom on how to live your life effectively. You have a community willing to help you and or comfort you in your time of distress. Whatever you decide to attach your spirit to, be sure that it is grounded in unconditional love, kindness, integrity, and wisdom.

"I would rather die believing in possibility than live believing that we are all here to be poor."

- Jim Stovall

Blind at 29, Best Selling Author & Speaker

Chapter 15

MIND, BODY, AND SPIRIT CHECKUP

"Never make a permanent decision based on a temporary situation".

- Bishop T.D. Jakes

Do you currently feel that your life is spinning out of control? Are your finances lacking? Are your parents, spouse, or children getting on your nerves? Are you considering a new job based on the fact that your current job doesn't pay you enough? Were you recently in a car accident? These types of situations can stress out most people very quickly. When this happens, you normally want to start to blame others for your situation. It's my spouses fault because he/she won't get a job making more money. It's my parents fault because they won't support my bad decisions and they won't loan me $1,000.00, although I know they have it. It's my supervisor's fault because they won't give me a raise and I've been working there for 5 years.

Because it is everyone else's fault, it will always be difficult for the situation to change, because you are waiting on someone else to change. You are the common denominator in all of these situations, so it is up to you to change. Are there situations that you can control? There are always situations that you can control, even if the only thing you are controlling is your perception of the situation. In other words, anything that makes you sad, angry or fearful is controlling your mind. Ask yourself this question:

"If I didn't believe it was impossible to have a life that was very fulfilling, what could I do?"

Now take an ACTION step toward doing just that, even in the absence of knowing everything. You have to take control of your own mind and not allow your current situation to stress you out. You have to go into the mode of,

"OK God, this is a really tough situation that I am in. What is the lesson here? What are you trying to teach me? I know if I don't see the lessons right now at this moment, it will be clear later in my life when I will need to refer back to this day."

This type of attitude will allow you to control your mind and your perception of what happens to you in life. Worry and fear is your perception of something that actually may never happen. It's important to calm down, relax, THINK, and then go into ACTION on how you will conquer this moment in your life, like you have done so many times in the past. Worry and fear are a total waste of time.

When these tough times in life occur, and they WILL occur, it is time to do a healthy mind, healthy body, and healthy spirit assessment. Lack in any of these areas will affect ALL of the other areas.

Healthy Mind Assessment:

Table 15-1

	1. Do you have problems falling asleep or staying asleep?
	2. Do you wake up between 2:30 – 3:00 am at least 3 nights per week?
	3. Do you lack energy to do the things that you normally enjoy?
	4. Do you ever feel down, depressed, or hopeless?
	5. Do you have thoughts of hurting yourself or hurting others?

Check all that apply over the past week.

If you checked off three of the five and/or #5, please call the number below immediately to talk about what is bothering you. They would love to talk to you about developing strong coping skills.

Boys Town Crisis Line (Adults and Children): 1-800-448-3000

Healthy Body Assessment:

Table 15-2

	1. Have you eliminated sodas, sweets, juices, from your diet?
	2. Are you eating your fruits and vegetables and/or supplementing your diet with vitamins and minerals?
	3. Are you doing cardio training 3 times per week?
	4. Are you doing weight training 2 times per week?
	5. Have you watched the movie "What the Health" on Netflix

Healthy Spirit Assessment:

Table 15-3

	1. Have you studied your spiritual guide based on your religious preference?
	2. Are you listening to music that uplifts the spirit inside of you? The songs should make your heart feel warm, make you cry, or give you goose bumps.
	3. Do you meditate/pray daily?

It is possible that you are malnourished. The great thing is that you now know what to do to get your life back in check. Doing things your way may not be working for you.

"Most people tiptoe their way through life, hoping they make it safely to death."

- Earl Nightingale

Chapter 16

FOLLOW THE DAILY ROUTINE OF SUCCESSFUL PEOPLE

"Our daily decisions and habits have a huge impact upon both our levels of happiness and success."

- Shawn Achor

Successful people are very systematic in their approach to life. They live life on purpose which helps to ensure that they get all of the things out of life that they want. Keeping a balance between having a healthy mind, a healthy body, and a healthy spirit is vital to live a stress-free life. Successful people watch very little television, they keep their goals and dreams in front of them, they sleep between 6 and 7 hours each night, they work out to relieve stress and anxiety, they show love and attention towards their family, and they ensure they are feeding their spirit.

Monday – Friday

The first 20 minutes of each day is devoted solely on developing a healthy SPIRIT.

1. *4:30 am:* Wake up after 6-7 hours of sleep.

2. *4:30 am – 4:50 am:* Spiritual Development (reading, listening, praying, meditating, etc.)

The next 18 minutes of each day is devoted solely on renewing your MIND. Waking up 36 minutes earlier is a small price to pay for the massive success you will experience in your life and your family

3. *4:50 am – 4:51 am:* Review your *Vision Board*

4. *4:51 am – 4:54 am:* Review your *Short-Term and Long-Term Goals*

5. *4:54 am – 4:56 am:* Recite your *Daily Affirmations*

6. *4:56 am – 5:06 am:* Meditate on your future through the *Visualization Exercise*

7. *5:06 am – 5:08 am:* Recite your *Gratefulness List*

The next 75 minutes is devoted to the renewing of your BODY through exercise, eating a healthy breakfast, and taking the necessary supplements to ensure you get the required vitamins and minerals your body needs each day

8. *5:15 am – 5:45 am:* Physical workout (i.e. running, weightlifting, etc.)

9. *5:45 am – 6:15 am:* Prepare for work or school

10. *6:15 am – 6:30 am:* Eat breakfast, take vitamin supplements, and have a conversation with your spouse & children (tell everyone that you love them).

11. *6:30 am – 7:00 am:* Travel to work/school

12. *7:00 am – 7:30 am:* Plan your day's activities, review all emails from the previous day to ensure you didn't miss anything.

13. *7:30 am:* Everyone else arrives to work/school

14. *7:30 am – 11:00 am:* Perform at a very high level at work/school. Give more than what you are paid or asked to give. Stay away from social media while at work/school as it is a waste of time. Be respectful and don't talk bad about others.

15. *11:00 am – 12:00 pm:* Lunch, check your social media sites, call/text your spouse

16. *12:00 pm – 4:00 pm:* Continue to perform at a very high level.

17. *4:00 pm – 4:30 pm:* Plan for tomorrow's work schedule and check emails from earlier in the day to ensure you didn't overlook anything. Return all promised phone calls for the day.

If you are a leader at work or in your community, make sure you understand that all subordinates want to know four things about their leader:

a) *Are You Committed?* You ask me to come to work on time, but you are always late.

b) *Can You Mentor Me?* I want to climb the ladder in this company and want to achieve what you have achieved. Can you meet with me one-on-one and show me how to navigate my career?

c) *Can I Trust You?* Can I trust that when I share personal information that you will keep my information close to you and not share it with others? Can I trust that you will protect me from senior leadership if I make a mistake, or will you *"throw me and the team under the bus"*?

d) ***Do You Care About Me?*** Do you know anything about me? Do you know I have three kids? Do you care? Did you know that my son is an accomplished violinist? Did you take the time to bring a card to the hospital when my spouse was sick?

A few of these leadership approaches were taught to me by one of my mentors, Chief Master Sergeant (ret.) Derrick Crowley at MacDill Air Force Base, FL, in 2011 and it has been a staple in my own leadership approach ever since. If your subordinates can answer YES to all four, they will follow you through a brick wall.

18. *4:30 pm – 5:15 pm:* Pick up children and/or make a grocery runs

19. *5:15 pm – 5:45 pm:* Travel home (call and catch up with friends and extended family while driving)

20. *5:45 pm – 6:00 pm:* Arrive home and wind down

21. *6:00 pm – 7:00 pm:* Spend time with children and help with homework

22. *7:00 pm – 8:00 pm:* Discuss your day with your spouse and eat dinner

23. *8:00 pm – 8:30 pm:* Watch one TV show with your spouse and put kids to bed

24. *8:30 pm – 9:30 pm:* Do homework for your college degree (Associates, Bachelor's Master's, or PhD)

25. *9:30 pm – 10:00 pm:* Go to bed

Friday Night Ideas

1. *6:00 pm - 10:00 pm:*

   - Dinner and a movie with spouse and kids

   - Date night with spouse

   - High school football game with family

   - One-on-one date night with one of the children (your spouse can take the other child), the kids can switch with the other parent on the following week.

It is important to spend individual time with ALL of your kids as they need their own personal relationship with each parent.

- Pizza party at home while watching a pay-to-view movie

- Game night (board games) with family and/or friends

- Take a walk in the park or the beach after dinner to talk about the future of your family

Saturday

1. *7:30 am – 8:00 am:* Wake up after 7-10 hours of sleep. Spiritual time, review your goals and your dream poster, and meditate on your future.

2. *8:00 am – 10:00 am:* Home improvement projects, hobbies, yard work, and/or house cleaning

3. *10:00 am – 10:30 am:* Family meeting to discuss prior week's achievements and family goals for next week...discuss field trips, school photos, science projects, school events, etc.

4. *10:30 am - 11:00 am:* Have a meeting with your spouse to discuss finances, investments, bills, vacations, upcoming house guests, requests by family members to borrow money, etc.

5. *11:00 am - 5:00 pm:* Attend children sporting events, hobbies, watch college sports, attend children's birthday parties, go to the beach, the carnival, do college homework, etc.

6. *5:00 pm – 7:00 pm:* Take a walk with your spouse, go to a dinner party with friends, family game night, etc.

7. *7:00 pm – 9:00 pm:* Relaxation in the man or woman cave... read the success book *Think and Grow Rich*, by Napoleon Hill, call a friend/sibling/parents to check on them, catch up on your recorded favorite TV shows, etc.

Sunday

1. *8:00 am:* Wake up after 7-10 hours of sleep. Spiritual time, review your goals and your dream poster, and meditate on your future.

2. *9:30 am – 10:30 am:* Get dressed for Sunday Service

3. *10:30 am – 11:00 am:* Travel to Sunday Service

4. *1:30 pm – until:* Read *Think and Grow Rich* (2 hours), then relax and rest.

Community Volunteerism

4x per month – Attend Kiwanis ® or Rotary Club ® Meetings

2x per month - Feed the homeless, mentor kids, speak to youth, read to the elderly, etc.

1x per month – Attend networking meetings to collaborate with successful people

1x per month – Attend fraternity, sorority, or masonic meetings

"Mentors provide professional networks, outlets for frustration, college and career counseling, general life advice, and most importantly, an extra voice telling a student they are smart enough and capable enough to cross the stage at graduation and land their first paycheck from a career pathway job".

- Gerald Chertavian

Chapter 17

DISCOVER YOUR DREAM CAREER

"A career is something that you train for and prepare for and plan on doing for a long time."

- Sonia Sotomayor

Chase is a dreamer and absolutely loves to cook. After many years of hearing everyone praise his cooking, he decided to attend the top culinary school in America, Le Cordon Bleu College in Atlanta, Georgia. After completing the rigorous, fast-paced course, he graduated at the top of his class. He was pretty excited and had won many accolades while in school.

He began working in a few high-end restaurants and earned the coveted title of Chef but did not like the politics involved in corporate America. He wanted to have the freedom to create his own signature dishes without going through a lengthy approval process and he didn't enjoy being micro-managed. He quickly sat down and wrote a business plan so that he can open his own restaurant. He used most of the information from a class project and new information from the internet to develop his business plan. In his business plan, he addressed his many years of cooking, his educational success, his demographics, his menu, his growth plan, and his finances.

Once his business plan was complete, he began looking for a way to finance his new venture. He needed $60,000 to purchase an existing small restaurant that was going out of business as well as have some monies available for food, supplies, salaries, and a small cushion for emergencies. He had applied for small business loans but was denied due to his lack of collateral. After getting really frustrated and praying that he does not lose the opportunity to purchase the small restaurant, he decided to go to his older brother for assistance. He had been really hesitant in asking his brother because his brother can be really aggressive and if he decides to invest, he will probably ask about his investment in the restaurant often and the Chef doesn't like to be pressured about finances.

The Chef presents his business plan to his older "Corporate" brother for review. His older brother praised him on a thorough business plan but made a few suggestions on what he felt would help his brother get approved for financing. One suggestion was to show how much capital the Chef was willing to invest in himself. *"Many times, investors want to know how much of your own money you are willing to invest in your dream,"* said the

"Corporate Brother." After the Corporate Brother made his suggestions, he got quiet for a moment. By the way, the Corporate Brother has a Master's Degree in Business Administration (MBA), his investments have paid off well for him, and he has a net worth of $5 million. He tells his younger brother, "I've decided to invest in you and I will give you $50,000 to start your restaurant. Let me help you negotiate the sales price with the seller of the restaurant, I'm sure we can get his price down, then pay half up-front and spread the other payments out over 18 months. I will also do your accounting for you because an entrepreneur must have proper accounting in place if they are to be successful."

The Chef was absolutely elated that his brother was willing to invest in his dream. He couldn't wait to get started, but first they both negotiated the purchase of the restaurant. The seller sold him the restaurant for $20,000 down and $1,000 per month for 25 months. The Chef opened his restaurant and immediately discovered it would cost more than his business plan had projected. He cut corners where he could but he knew he had to get open very quickly.

After being opened for four weeks, the Corporate Brother decided to come by for a visit. When he walked up to the building, he was looking around and noticed that there was no sign outside, just a small banner that read "Restaurant Now Open." He walked into the front door and looked over to the left and noticed there was some small specs of food on the floor, then he looked to the right and noticed a few small rips in the carpet. As he continued looking around the restaurant, he noticed the tablecloths did not match and were not of nice quality. The Corporate Brother walked into the small employee break area and noticed that the time clock was broken and employees were writing in their times on their time cards. He said to himself, *"my little brother sure does trust his employees not to lie about their work hours"*. He spoke to one of the employees who told him that he was frustrated because two people called-in and won't make it to work, leaving the serving staff at 50% manned.

The Corporate Brother had seen enough and was very concerned with how his brother was running the business. He felt as though his brother was focusing too much on the cooking aspect of the restaurant and not on the operational aspect of the business. He decided to approach his brother about his assessment of the business operations. He walked into the kitchen and the music volume was slightly elevated, the Chef was singing, dancing, and cooking. He was truly enjoying himself and living out his dream. The kitchen area was very clean and the pots and pans were shiny and well maintained.

The corporate brother approached him and said *"Brother, I'm concerned about how you are running your business. There are a lot of things that need your attention and you are just focusing on cooking and leading your kitchen staff. As a business owner, you should be thinking strategically, thinking about the big operational picture as you plan the future of* your business". The Chef said, *"Brother, I'm not an operational guy, I am a Chef and this is what I love to do and what I'm going to do. You are an operational, corporate thinker, so roll up your sleeves, jump in and help me. If I asked you to come in here and cook, you would be totally lost. With that said, I have no desire to be an operational leader of this business. I only want to cook, but you can jump in at any time."* The corporate brother was taken aback by his comments as he thought his brother was prepared to "DO IT ALL" when he said he wanted to be an entrepreneur. He realized at that moment that his brother did not have the desire to lead others and that his brother was a creative thinker with big dreams but needed his own corporate experience and personality to become his business partner to take the business to a new level. The corporate brother said to himself, *"I can TALK about change, or I can BE the change I want to see"*, so he tells his younger brother that he will take care of those things.

The corporate brother arranged for the floors to be cleaned, new carpet installed, high quality tablecloths that added to the décor were placed on all of the tables, and the time clock was repaired. One of the servers was promoted to Head Server and one of their duties was to manage everyone's schedule and keep at least one server on standby each day. The corporate brother also purchased new uniforms for the entire staff. He went outside and had a very nice sign put on the building. He created an intense marketing campaign that included social media, TV commercials, and print ads in magazines and newspapers. Within the first 6 months of the restaurant opening, business had increased by 500% and customers were extremely pleased.

Please pause and take the story in and ask yourself these questions, *"Which of the brothers more closely match my own desires to be the leader or the creative mind? Am I the Chef or am I Corporate?* As you ponder your position in this story, please understand that both brothers were absolutely necessary to ensure the restaurant's success. Most of the time, it will take two people with opposite personalities to help a business, institution, corporation, or military organization become successful.

I'm sure you have heard the term *"opposites attract,"* I would change that to say *"opposites complete each other"*.

When running a small organization, there are a lot of things that need to be done in order to make the business a success. Can the Chef truly make the most delicious and delectable food, and run an efficient and effective kitchen if he is also worrying about marketing, human resources, training, payroll, hiring, customer service, etc.? He needed help and he needed the right help, not another personality like his own who may find an area like marketing and only focus on that. The Chef needed someone who could see the big picture and then not be afraid to execute quickly with confidence.

There are many lessons that could be taught in the story...leadership, teamwork, personal relationships, aspects of entrepreneurship, personality differences, etc. This entire section was pulled from a leadership book that I am writing but can be used here to show the difference in personalities and to help people, especially young people focus on a career and truly build something amazing. Many people can get very confused and not know what they want to do with their lives. So, they either attempt to please everyone who will exploit their talents and their kindness, or they will spend their lives chasing money and success, only to one day wake up and realize they are behind on their goals and their dreams.

Being a Chef or Corporate has absolutely nothing to do with your education or intellect, but it has everything to do with your natural abilities to do what you enjoy. You may be thinking, well I am definitely a Chef, or I am definitely Corporate. You may also scratch your head and think that you may be in the middle. If you are in the middle, then you would be considered a Chef. Corporate people are aggressive and highly driven to succeed and they know it.

I must take a moment to introduce a third brother. We will call him the "Engineering Brother." The engineering brother was hired to fix everything in the restaurant. He repairs the freezer, stoves, light fixtures, electrical systems, etc. If he is faced with a challenge, he will keep at it until he figures it out. He is highly focused on the task at hand, prefers to work alone, doesn't say a lot, and always has tools in his hand. He is an introvert who loves solving problems that most people consider complex or tedious. He comes to work on-time and leaves at exactly 5:00 pm each day.

Take a look at the charts on the following pages. They are designed to help young people and older people figure out which category they fit-in to decide what they may be good at. If the story didn't help you figure out if you are an engineer, chef, or corporate person, then the charts below should help by looking at the hobbies of each, then deciding if a career choice that has interested you is on the chart. This was designed to help you lock-in on what is a more natural choice to focus on when starting a business, joining the military, or joining corporate America. If you still say none of the three choices fit your professional personality, then you are most likely an engineer because some engineers don't like to be categorized, forcing you to resist this entire exercise.

The earlier we lock in on our future, the more successful our lives will be. So, use the career charts on the following pages to continue to find and live your dream!

Chart 17-1

ENGINEER

Professional Career Choices – Engineer

Engineer (i.e. Mechanical, Chemical, Civil, Electrical, Software, etc.)	Entertainment industry: Sound & music production / Singer / Dancer
Scientist / Surgeon	Clothing Designer
Computer Security/Information Assurance	Construction
Ethical Hacker	Science Fiction Author
Web Designer	Military Special Forces and Bomb Disposal
Mechanic	Painter / Artist
Marine Biologist	Military Intelligence
Central Intelligence Agency (CIA)	Federal Bureau of Investigations (FBI)
Landscaping	Philanthropist (gives away money)
Veterinarian	Dentist
Attorney (i.e. Corporate, Family Law, etc.)	Anthropologist / Biologist

Hobbies – Engineer

Rebuilding and tinkering w/antique cars	Martial Arts
Sewing and Knitting	Unethical hacking
Golf	Fishing
Home improvement projects	Extreme Computing and/or Gaming
Trading Cards / Comics	Sci-Fi
Writing	Drawing / Painting / Photography
Model Cars / Planes	Chess
Reading	Rocketry
Investing	Archery

If you identify with an Engineer, select careers that match your interest

Chart 17-2

CHEF or "Creative Entrepreneur"

Professional Career Choices – Chef

College Professor	Community Activists/Social Worker
School Teacher	Cosmetology/Barber
Military Professional: Healthcare / Computer Tech Administration / Chapel Services / Logistics / Pilot Public Affairs / Human Resources / Mechanic	Professional Athlete: Football / Basketball Baseball / Golf / Boxer
Entertainer: Musician/Actor/Artist/Performer	Entrepreneur / Non-profit business owner
Pastor	Construction
Healthcare: Doctor / Psychologist / Nurse / Lab Tech	Engineers: Computer / Electrical / Civil Construction / Chemical / Architects
Fashion Designer / Interior Designer	Culinary Arts
Multi-level Marketing / Direct Sales	Florist
Athletic Coach	Financial Advisor/Insurance Agent

Hobbies - Chef

Church Volunteer	Play musical instruments
Involvement in fraternal/civic organizations	Coaching youth activities/sports
Small business on the side	Mentoring
Community activist	Gardening, home improvement projects
Drawing and designing for a future clothing line	Cooking / Grilling / Baking with dreams of owning a restaurant
Watching HGTV 3 hours or more per day	Social Media enthusiast
Antique collection and repurpose projects	Works with homeless and downtrodden
Happy to care for ill/elderly family members	Fast cars, motorcycle riding, biking
Singing / Dancing / Acting	Video Gaming
Trading Cards and Comics	Sci-Fi
Outdoors: Skiing / watersports / Snowboarding	Watching reality TV cooking shows
Sports: Basketball / Football / Baseball	Bodybuilding / Running

If you identify with a Chef, select careers that match your interest

Chart 17-3

CORPORATE or "Heroic Leader / Field General"

Professional Career Choices – Corporate

Police officer/ Police Supervisor / Police Chief	Marketing Manager / Marketing Director
Fire person / Fire Inspector / Fire Chief	Director of Sales / Training / Human Res.
Military Officer and Non-Commissioned Officer	Executive Director for Community and Non-Profit Organizations
Entrepreneurial Partner	Judge
Corporate Executive	Project Manager / Program Manager
Fast Food Management	Investor / Stock Broker
Entertainment Industry Executive	Retail Management
Information Technology Management	Commercial / Military Pilot
Attorney	Construction Foreman
Doctor Who Owns Multiple Clinics	Postal Worker
Logistics Manager	Nurse Anesthetist

Hobbies – Corporate

Investing	Martial Arts
Real Estate	Swimming
Billiards	Traveling
Hunting	Basketball, Softball, Weightlifting, Running
Coaching and Mentoring	Sports Fan
Volunteering	Bowling

If you identify with Corporate, select careers that match your interest

"Success is no accident. It is hard work, perseverance, learning, studying, sacrifice and most of all, love of what you are doing or learning to do."

- Pele

SUCCESS TOOLS

TOOL # 1
EMERGENCY REFERRAL SERVICES

The referral information below is for use by parents, teachers, mentors, and children. Teenagers, please use the information to help your friends and family members in need. Our friends will reach out to us in time of crisis and usually we don't know what to tell them to do. Now we know where to send them.

Nationwide 24-Hour Hotline

Alcohol and Drug Abuse

National Drug Information Treatment and Referral Hotline...............1-800-662-HELP (4357)
Drug Hotline...1-800-333-4313

Local:	
Local:	

Family and Individual Crisis Hotline

Boys Town Suicide and Crisis Line (Adults and Children) 1-800-448-3000
National Youth Crisis Hotline...1-800-442-HOPE (4673)
Suicide Hotline...1-800-333-4313
Covenant House Hotline...1-800-999-9999

Local:	
Local:	

Sexual Assault / Rape, Child Abuse and Domestic Violence

RAINN National Rape Crisis Hotline.. 1-800-656-HOPE (4673)
National Child Abuse Hotline... 1-800-25-ABUSE (22873)
Childhelp USA... 1-800-422-4453
National Domestic Violence Hotline...................................... 1-800-799-SAFE (7233)

Local:	
Local:	

Crisis Counseling and Services for Runaways

National Runaway Switchboard... 1-800-621-4000

Local:	

TOOL # 2
STUDY SUCCESS

SUCCESSFUL PEOPLE TO WATCH AND STUDY

1. Steve Harvey
2. Bob Proctor
3. Warren Buffett
4. Tony Robbins
5. Jim Rohn
6. T.D. Jakes
7. Joel Osteen
8. Eric Thomas

MOVIES TO WATCH AND STUDY

1. *The Secret,* 2006, Rated PG, Director: Drew Heriot
2. **Coach Carter**, 2005, Rated PG-13, Director: Thomas Carter
3. *The Pursuit of Happyness*, 2006, Rated PG-13, Director: Gabriele Muccino
4. *Good Will Hunting*, 1997, Rated R, Director: Gus Van Sant
5. *Pay it Forward*, 2000, Rated PG-13, Director: Mimi Leder
6. *The Blind Side*, 2009, Rated PG-13, Director: John Lee Hancock
7. *Remember the Titans*, 2000, Rated PG, Director: Boaz Yakin
8. *Rudy*, 1993, Rated PG, Director: David Anspaugh

Deeper Dive into Law of Attraction - Powerful Lessons in Wealth and Abundance

1. *Think and Grow Rich, The Legacy,* 2017, Rated PG, Director: Scott Cervine
2. *Beyond the Secret—Law of Attraction (YouTube),* 2009, Rated PG, Director: Holli Walker
3. **The MetaPhysical Secret-Law of Attraction (YouTube)**

REFERENCES

[01] Tad James Company, 2016, Neurolinguistic Programming, http://www.nlpcoaching.com/

[02] College Choice, 2018, 50 Highest Paying Careers for College Graduates, https://www.collegechoice.net/50-highest-paying-careers-college-graduates/

[03] Monster, 2018, The 10 Highest-Paying Health Care Jobs, https://www.monster.com/career-advice/article/top-10-health-care-jobs-salary

[04] Nurse.Org, 2017, 15 Highest Paying Nursing Careers, https://nurse.org/articles/15-highest-paying-nursing-careers/

[05] Types of Engineering Degrees, 2018, Highest Paid Engineering Jobs, https://typesofengineeringdegrees.org/highest-paid-engineering-jobs/

[06] The Balance Careers, 2018, The Highest Paying Legal Jobs, https://www.thebalancecareers.com/highest-paying-legal-jobs-2164341

[07] Study.Com, 2018, Highest Paying Jobs in the Video Game Industry, https://study.com/articles/highest_paying_jobs_in_the_video_game_industry.html

[08] Defense Finance and Accounting Service, 2018, Military Pay Charts 1949-2018, https://www.dfas.mil/militarymembers/payentitlements/military-pay-charts.html

[09] The Collaborative for Academic, Social, and Emotional Learning, 2018, https://casel.org/

[10] PsychCentral®, 2017, Michael Akers & Grover Porter, What is Emotional Intelligence (EQ)? https://psychcentral.com/lib/what-is-emotional-intelligence-eq/

[11] Centers for Disease Control and Prevention, 2017, Healthy Weight, https://www.cdc.gov/healthyweight

CONTACT US

Training Courses for Students (Age 10 to 30-years-old)

One-on-One Coaching with Rod Cunningham

Train-the-Trainer Certification Courses

- ★ Mentors
- ★ City Youth Directors
- ★ Non-Profit Staff Dealing with Youth
- ★ Adoption Agencies
- ★ Social Workers
- ★ School Detention Teachers
- ★ Veterans Affairs/PTSD Hotline Employees

Speaking Engagements

- ★ Colleges
- ★ Police Departments
- ★ Youth Groups
- ★ Prisons/Juvenile Detention Centers
- ★ Schools
- ★ Parents
- ★ Teachers/Counselors
- ★ Veterans Affairs/PTSD Hotline Employees

Info@rodcunninghamspeaks.com

www.rodcunninghamspeaks.com

Made in the USA
Columbia, SC
16 February 2023

12384863R00102